Media Is Us

Media Is Us

Understanding Communication and Moving beyond Blame

Elizaveta Friesem

ROWMAN & LITTLEFIELD
Lanham • Boulder • New York • London

Published by Rowman & Littlefield
An imprint of The Rowman & Littlefield Publishing Group, Inc.
4501 Forbes Boulevard, Suite 200, Lanham, Maryland 20706
www.rowman.com

6 Tinworth Street, London SE11 5AL, United Kingdom

British Library Cataloguing in Publication Information Available

Library of Congress Cataloging-in-Publication Data on File

Names: Friesem, Elizaveta, author.
Title: Media is us : understanding communication and moving beyond blame /
    Elizaveta Friesem.
Description: Lanham : Rowman & Littlefield, [2021] | Includes bibliographical
    references and index. | Summary: "Exploring the nature of modern media,
    Friesem uses the fundamental principles of human communication to move
    away from the fear and blame that usually accompany discussions of new media
    technologies. The book employs the ACE model (from Awareness to Collaboration
    through Empathy) to build media literacy across professions and academic
    disciplines" — Provided by publisher.
Identifiers: LCCN 2021014645 (print) | LCCN 2021014646 (ebook) |
    ISBN 9781538150511 (cloth) | ISBN 9781538174074 (pbk) |
    ISBN 9781538150528 (ebook)
Subjects: LCSH: Mass media—Social aspects. | Communication—Social aspects. |
    Blame. | Power (Social sciences) | Empathy.
Classification: LCC HM1206 .F75 2021 (print) | LCC HM1206 (ebook) |
    DDC 302.23—dc23
LC record available at https://lccn.loc.gov/2021014645
LC ebook record available at https://lccn.loc.gov/2021014646

To Yonty, Robin, and Sky

Only the paradox comes anywhere near to comprehending the fullness of life. Non-ambiguity and non-contradiction are one-sided and thus unsuited to express the incomprehensible.

Carl Jung

Contents

Acknowledgments

Any big project is a result of collaboration between multiple individuals; Even a project like this book, which involved a lot of solitary reading, writing, and editing. Many of the people who helped me to make this manuscript happen may never know about it. Perhaps surprisingly, I myself won't know all of their names. I tend to agree with the French philosopher Roland Barthes, who believed that no author can really understand how culture and language speak through her. No matter how hard I try, I would not be able to list every contributor whose words and actions influenced this volume. Those whom I could think of are included here and in the bibliography.

Since I am such an introvert, only a few friends of mine ever found out that I was working on this book. I am grateful to all people who asked me about it and said some encouraging words, including Sahana, Urszula, Gabi, Sergio and Lizzy, Kelsey, Noni and David, Tanya and Val, Zoey and Geoffrey, Cynthia and Jay, Morgan Jaffe, Masha Mogilevich, Jana Romanova, Mary O'Connor, Bert Mitchell, Gus Andrews, Sharon Bloyd-Peshkin, Jenn Midberry, and Susan Messer. (I included last names in instances where I felt that they were necessary for my friends to identify themselves.) More specifically, Sahana and Gabi, both so far away from me geographically, inquired about my progress multiple times, which I really appreciate; Morgan Jaffe edited the first draft of my first chapter; Gus Andrews shared insights about stages of the publishing processes; Susan Messer encouraged me by talking about her experiences of being a published author, and Sharon Bloyd-Peshkin helped me navigate my book contract. I am afraid I may be forgetting names of a few friends with whom I had brief conversations about the book along the way. I hope they will forgive me!

Special thanks go to Andrey Koshelev and Renee Hobbs, as well as to Garry Cooper. Renee has been my mentor in the field of media literacy for a number of years and boosted my self-confidence as I was learning to be a writer. I am also grateful for the tremendous help she provided by being my supporter as I was looking for a place to publish this book. Online conversations with Andrey helped me feel that I was not alone as I was working through some of the most challenging parts of the manuscript. During our meandering Messenger chats, he shared his insights about many different issues and sent links to thought-provoking sources. Last but not least, I want to thank Garry for asking great questions about my creative process, for showing interest in the ideas I developed in this volume, and for repeatedly pointing out the importance of my work. Thank you, Garry!

When I finally had the courage to start looking for a place to publish the manuscript, Elizabeth Swayze was the editor who believed in this project. Unfortunately, she had to step down soon after offering me the contract. Once that happened, Natalie Mandziuk guided me along the rest of the publishing process. I am grateful to Elizabeth and Natalie for their support, patience, and organizational skills.

My parents Olga and Nicolay have played a major role in the creation of this work by encouraging me to become an intellectually curious person that I am now. In the recent years, they asked me multiple times about the progress of my book. Having both parents' support is one of the most important things that one can ask for to have a fulfilling life. Special thanks go to my maternal grandfather, Nicolay Mirniy, who taught me with his example to be detail-oriented and organized in my work and helped me to develop my love for reading.

Finally, this book would not be possible without conscious and unconscious contributions from my husband Yonty and my two sons: Robin and Sky. Yonty and I have many things in common, and we have also plenty of differences. Sometimes, he has been the devil's advocate; on other occasions, he challenged my opinions. But more often than not, he has supported me by generously sharing concepts and sources that I used to develop my ideas. It is thanks to him that I started to explore media literacy and realized that empathy can be enhanced. This book would not be possible without him. At the time this manuscript is being prepared for publication, Robin and Sky have no clue about it, because they don't care much for books without pictures. They also don't know how often they provide me with opportunities to practice empathy and nonviolent communication! Indeed, it is by observing how they grow and learn that I have been able to gain some important insights about the human nature. Most importantly, when I feel stuck for some reason, there is nothing better than a snuggle with the two little devils to remind me that life is beautiful.

Introduction

A few years ago, I was scrolling down my Facebook news feed when my eyes paused on an image shared by a friend. It was a screenshot collage from an ad for Dove body wash. Thanks to the post accompanying the image, my mind became immediately fixated on one fact: the picture appeared to show a Black woman transitioning into a light-skinned redhead. What I saw looked like a "before" and "after" kind of commercial, although a smiling young model was removing her shirt to reveal a completely different person (also wearing a shirt).

My friend's disapproving comment and the article her link led to immediately shaped my interpretation of the ad as overtly racist. It seemed that Dove was suggesting that their body wash can turn a Black person into a White one! Having studied the history of media representations, I could see troubling parallels with the time when saying that darker skin is dirty was acceptable and even entertaining (for some people, at least).[1] "What is going on here?" I was wondering as I typed the phrase "Dove racist ad" into the Google search bar. Numerous articles discussing racial insensitivity immediately popped up.[2]

Back then, I still used my online social networks to find out what was going on in the world and to share my opinions. The story I stumbled upon called for a reaction. I could not believe that racial bias was so explicitly embedded in a present-day ad for the famous personal care brand. And yet the evidence was there. So many people were talking about it! Even the big media outlets that I had learned to trust featured commentaries condemning Dove's misstep. My verdict came swiftly: the campaign was unacceptable.

Feeling compelled to share my observations with others, I chose one of the articles and posted it on my Facebook wall together with the following text: "Wow, this new Dove ad is outrageous! I was naïve to think that the idea of comparing 'Black' with dirt and 'White' with cleanliness is gone. Clearly, some people still embrace it, and those who work at Dove did not learn about nuances of racial representation." I made my post public in order to spread the word.

About fifteen minutes later, three comments from people I did not know appeared underneath the post. None of their authors was hostile, but they clearly did not agree with my point of view. Two responses were sarcastic: "Whatever you say" and "If this ad exists, it must be racist." I was ready to dismiss them as coming from someone who did not understand nuances of media portrayals. Yet the third comment was longer, and it made me pause. A stranger wrote: "Why do you think it has something to do with comparing dirt to cleanliness? Did you see the whole ad? After the second person removes her shirt, she turns into an Asian girl. This ad represents different races. If they had the transformation happen in the other direction, would you be happy or would you still think the ad is racist?"

I felt chills running down my spine. Did I just screw up? After all, I had not done much research before jumping on the bandwagon of blame. Taking a deep breath, I googled the story again. One of the links led to the whole video, which was a 3-second GIF featuring three women. It was not a story of a Black model turning into a White one, as the screenshot collage everybody was discussing implied. The redhead also removed her shirt to reveal what to me looked like a Hispanic woman with slightly darker skin and black hair.

Then I discovered something even more interesting. Lola Ogunyemi, the first model in the GIF sequence, spoke to news outlets defending Dove's creative decision. She explained that the snippet posted on the company's Facebook wall was a teaser for a longer TV commercial that was supposed to feature seven women of various ethnic backgrounds. The idea was to emphasize the beauty of diversity, and Lola had been excited to be part of this campaign. At no point during the process did she feel any implication that one skin shade was presented as superior to others. "I am not just some silent victim of a mistaken beauty campaign. I am strong, I am beautiful, and I will not be erased," Lola Ogunyemi told *The Guardian*.[3] Yet the erasure of her voice was evident when so many online commentators told the story without citing the person whose face was in the center of the controversy.

This experience left me embarrassed, frustrated, and sad. I was embarrassed because, as a person claiming to be media literate, I should have known better. Frustration came from the suspicion that many good people saw the body wash ad as undeniably racist. Finally, I was sad because I did not know how to change the situation and because I was afraid to share my true opinion through social media. My suspicion was that friends from my liberal filter bubble would not have appreciated it if I had suggested that the ad was not that racist after all. And I hate to have arguments online, where I cannot see the other person's body language or use my own nonverbal cues to make the conversation friend-lier. Dealing with all these negative emotions was not fun. But soon it felt bet-ter. At that time, I had been working on this book for a year and a half, and the experience with the ad was a perfect way to introduce my ideas.

First, I was writing about people's relationship with media and my point was that we should shift the focus to exploring our interactions with each other and deepen our understanding of ourselves. In the recent years, concerns about fake news have been on the rise. I am troubled by the fact that most of the conversations about this phenomenon focus on misinformation or disinformation that "other people" (manipulative or biased) produce to confuse "people like us" (good but sometimes naïve). The story about the Dove ad became another reminder that the "us vs. them" binary is not helpful when we are trying to make sense of how media works.[4]

Second, I wanted to talk about the trap we routinely fall in by making judgments about media (or *anything*, for that matter) in a rush. It was scary to realize how easy it was for me to start blaming Dove for being racist after doing some superficial online research and relying on my friends' reactions. On the other hand, once my mistake became apparent, the flood of new negative emotions threatened to shift the focus of my blame onto a new target: people from my own bubble who confused me, media outlets that were collectively crying wolf, and myself for not being more careful with my conclusions. I intuitively felt that blaming was not right, whoever the target might have been, and I wanted to explain this intuition to myself and others.

Third, the book was becoming really personal. I started writing it to share essential truths I had discovered but ended up inviting my readers to accompany me on my highly subjective intellectual journey. Everything I had to offer was only my interpretation, my version of the story. Same is the Dove ad tale I just told you.

A part of me resisted this approach. On some level, sounding unsure about my findings did not seem particularly appealing. Quite simply, I was afraid that my readers would not take me seriously. What helped me to find my voice and the courage to use it was the idea of vulnerability developed by Brené Brown.[5] Having decided to embrace imperfections of my insights, I gave myself permission not to be the all-knowing author. In fact, the argument that any truth is partial by definition yet still worth sharing became a cornerstone of my book.

WHAT SHOULD I EXPECT?

As any reader opening a new volume you must be asking yourself this question. If you do research or teach about media, the first thing you should know is that it is not a media studies or media literacy book—not in the traditional sense, at least. I do start it by asking questions about communication mediated by technology. I also provide a brief overview of the relevant history of thought (from a specific perspective that serves my goals). However, toward the middle of the first chapter, the focus shifts to include angles that are usually absent in academic and educational books on the same topic.

I suggest that, if we look at technology broadly—as a set of tools and techniques developed for a certain purpose—it may turn out that media has existed much longer than we tend to think. I formulate principles of communication that are meant to help us understand how people learn and interact, whether technology is involved or not—and no matter what kind of technology it is. This leads me to discuss what is so unique in interactions between people and how this uniqueness is related to what it means to be human. Exploring the principles of communication, I tackle such intimidating concepts as truth and power. One of my big claims is that in order to better understand media, we need to understand ourselves. And the other way around: if we become more self-aware about the way we see the world and act in it, this may increase our awareness of how other people communicate using technology.

For better or worse, I am a scholar of media. So if you are not one, you may think that this book is not for you. I hope that my subjective exploration will be interesting not only for people from my community but also for any college-educated curious reader who enjoys interdisciplinary intellectual adventures. I won't lie to you: this book gets abstract and philosophical more than once. Although the matters explored on the following pages are complex, I hope that simple language and engaging examples will make this volume sufficiently accessible. My motivation should be relevant beyond academia: to use the conversation about media for exploring strategies to diminish the current political and cultural polarization. The general idea I propose is not entirely new. I believe that we should use self-awareness to increase our empathy and learn to collaborate with each other despite differences of opinions. Nevertheless, you may find building blocks of my argument intriguing and see their combination as original.

Without further ado, here is how the book is structured.

Chapter 1 presents the starting point of my intellectual journey, which began by questioning the common understanding of media. A few theories are summarized in order to justify a need for a new definition and explain my issue with the language we use to talk about this phenomenon. At this point, the resemblance to a traditional book in media studies or media literacy ends. The readers will be introduced to five fundamental principles of human communication. These are meant to draw parallels between the way people learned from and connected with each other in the past and the way they do it now, when the latest technologies can fit into their pocket. I argue that the basis of communication has not changed and that understanding it will help us make sense of challenges we face in the modern society.

Chapter 2 invites the reader to take a step back in order to see media as part of the bigger picture. New cultural forms appear all the time, but the fundamental principles of human communication persist. Why? Because of the way our brains work, which is at the same time amazing and imperfect. Also because of how we make sense of the world around us, which can be explained by looking into uniquely human cognitive processes. I will challenge my readers with the idea of multiple truths by suggesting that each one of us has only partial access to what is called "reality." (As a side note, this does not mean that we must uncritically accept relativism or give up on any attempts to find a common language with each other.) Drawing on the theories of symbolic interactionism and the social construction of reality, I argue that by communicating, people create multiple realities they inhabit while these realities are simultaneously shaping ideas in people's own heads. This claim has a direct connection to the current debates about media, fueled by the concern about the way it can construct our perception of ourselves and others.

Chapter 3 may be the most challenging one to get through for multiple reasons. I use it to address the issue of power, which inevitably comes up when people are discussing the role that media plays in their lives. Power is a sensitive topic. This concept is essential for understanding social problems, yet it can conceal complexity of interactions between human beings. I use insights of such thinkers as Foucault to offer my own theory of power. This theory is meant to explain why it is unproductive to blame anybody for what's wrong with the social system, where everything is connected in most intricate ways. To further explain my understanding of power, I discuss the dependence of the social system on the interplay of stability and change, which constantly finds manifestations in the way we communicate. This chapter provides the final stepping stone that leads to one of the main arguments of the book: we need to overcome the widespread tendency to blame media—whether understood as objects or people—for imperfections of the human society.

Chapter 4 develops this argument by clarifying how blame works and offering alternatives. In contrast with the previous chapter, this one is not theoretical but personal; however, the conversation keeps being sensitive. After all, I argue that we should not blame media for whatever we think is wrong with our culture (e.g., fake news, polarization, consumerism). I am not trying to shame my readers for being angry, sad, or frustrated about social problems. My hope is that the insights about human communication and power relations from the previous chapters will be sufficient to justify the change of perspective I am proposing. We can use our negative emotions as indicators of issues that need to be addressed, but we should take our global interconnectedness into consideration as we are searching for solutions. Beyond blame lies empathy, which can allow us to have healthy curiosity about realities and truths different from ours. And communication can provide bridges between the worlds we live in. My hope is that empathy and the enhanced understanding of social complexity will help more people find ways to cross ideological divides and work toward a better society together.

Chapter 5 offers a practical model based on the arguments developed in the book. It is called ACE: from Awareness to Collaboration through Empathy. First, I describe my favorite strategy from media literacy education and encourage readers to analyze different types of media by themselves. Activities explained in the section on awareness are meant to increase understanding of taken-for-granted practices and of ideas surrounding us in our everyday lives. But awareness can lead to anger, frustration, fear, and passivity if it's not handled properly. I describe a strategy called nonviolent communication that can help us use empathy as a counterbalance for all these negative feelings. Finally, I lay out my argument for the need for collaboration that would be based on awareness and empathy of the highest order.

As you can see from this description, my book is very ambitious—too ambitious, perhaps. It starts with the search for a new definition of media and ends with the call for embracing our common responsibility for the world our children will inherit. I make everything boil down to communication—it's what we do all the time!—but then work hard to complicate my readers' perception of obvious everyday activities and objects. Using conversations about media in order to better understand ourselves and the human society, the volume moves toward my overarching goal. My hope is that this work will contribute to decreasing the current polarization by helping people see each other as pieces of a puzzle, not adversaries in the great debate on moral standards and best practices.

WHO'S THE AUTHOR ANYWAY?

Asking questions about people behind *any* ideas you encounter is essential. Same is true for being curious about the context where and when these ideas are communicated to you. It does not matter whether you are learning from your parents or peers, looking for information online, watching news, or reading a book. That is why, in the final part of the introduction I want to tell readers a bit about myself and my motivations for working on this project. Mind you, it is going to be only a very short and simplified account. Not to mention subjective. By revealing (what I consider to be) my main biases, I hope to prepare you for what is to come—or to spare you some time in case you decide that this author is not a person you'd be interested in hearing from.

I was born in the Soviet Union eight years before it fell apart. My parents, both middle-class and college-educated, wanted me to become an intellectual. They succeeded and overachieved their goal as I ended up studying for twenty-three years in total: eleven at school, then eight at St. Petersburg State University finishing with a Russian equivalent of a PhD, then four more years after I moved to the United States to get a doctoral degree in Media and Communication at Temple University, Philadelphia. By the end of this run, I wanted to be a media literacy educator helping people understand how ideologies (values, beliefs, assumptions) work through communication and how they can do harm.

Back in Russia, I was taught to use such disciplines as philosophy, sociology, anthropology, linguistics, history, and psychology to ask profound questions about the human-made world. Some writings we were discussing in class seemed so abstract and unnecessarily complicated that at some point I needed to take a break in order to decide what to do next. I discovered media studies and then media literacy purely by accident (long story) and was excited to work on questions that felt both more specific and applicable than: "What is culture?"

But the more I explored real-world issues associated with media, the more I wanted to go back to asking fundamental questions about the structure of society and the human nature. At the same time, I made a decision to talk about abstract ideas in the most accessible way possible (from my point of view, at least). Four years in the second doctoral program determined my preoccupation with issues of communication. This new direction became a professional deformation of sorts. Wherever I look, I see people communicating: exchanging information, sharing ideas, learning, and connecting with each other. Not surprisingly, these processes became the focus of my current exploration.

There is an even bigger bias shaping my work that must be addressed here. I am an optimist who wants to believe in people and in the power of human connection. Just to clarify, I do get annoyed and constantly judge others same as everybody else does. This is just how the human brain works. Yet, I have found that maintaining all kinds of relationships is easier when I don't assume bad intent and don't allow my judgments to guide my actions (as much as it's possible). This may be some sort of mental preservation mechanism. Over the years, I have kept finding out more and more about creative ways human beings have for tormenting each other. I often feel discouraged, but it has always helped me to think that deep underneath everybody is meant to be good. Not sure when and how this idea was imprinted in my mind, but it definitely took a long time to get fully articulated. Once I started looking deeper into the idea of empathy, which only happened when I moved to the United States, it was like "Bingo!"

The importance of empathy is basically my faith, an assumption I prefer not to question, same as other people do not question the existence of God. You will find this bias permeating my book, especially when I argue for the need to listen to others with an open mind and heart—even people we see as our enemies. I know very well that some readers will not agree with my core belief. And yet I decided to write the book this way, because this is my truth.

Speaking of truths: back in Russia, I discovered my tendency to mediate between friends with very different points of view. I am actually conflict averse, so jumping in the middle of an argument as a referee is totally not my thing. However, I remember marginally participating in quite a few heated online discussions with friends and formulating here and there in my comments why both sides had a point. Whenever I observe a debate—be it in person or online—I look for arguments that make sense to me no matter who they are coming from. It felt like a disadvantage for a while, like I could not decide whom to support. Then came a comforting thought: what if I am just looking for a balance? What if the bigger truth lies in some kind of combination of contradictory positions? Not a simple 2+2=4 kind of math, but something far more complex. This paradox provided a nice spot for the idea of empathy. If everybody is a bit right and a bit wrong at the same time, the first step toward overcoming disagreement would be to listen to each other's perspectives with patience, curiosity, and kindness.

The equation looked better this way, yet there was an element that did not seem to fit anywhere, and it was bothering me a lot: power. Many authors of trustworthy books and articles recommended by my professors were connecting social problems to bad choices of privileged social groups, including men, Whites, rich, able-bodied, and heterosexuals. This seemed logical. If society has problems, and if some people have more power than others, then the problems can be explained by actions of those in power. Why don't they use it to make the world better for everybody? Explanation: they must be mean, stupid, insensitive, plagued with biases, you name it. In this case, using empathy to communicate with these individuals or social groups they belong to would be a waste of time. But empathy is my faith, and I needed it to make sense even under these circumstances.

As all these ideas were combining and recombining in my head, the confirmation bias was doing its magic. I was diligently looking for evidence to confirm my beliefs and did eventually find them, as it always happens. Inspiration came from authors that talk about the importance of empathy and limitations of blame: Marshall Rosenberg, Brené Brown, and Martin Luther King Jr. have become significant influences. Michel Foucault's ideas about power, Peggy McIntosh's fluid privilege, theories of symbolic interactionism, social construction of reality, and the postmodernist claim that objective truth is not accessible to individual human brain provided further support for my thinking processes.

In my mind, I have been cataloging examples of paradoxes associated with human beings and their ways: violent yet sensitive and empathic; equipped with wondrous brains filled with hidden glitches; curious about new things but fearful of change. Following Carl Jung, I am convinced that "only the paradox comes anywhere near to comprehending the fullness of life."[6] Trying to get to the bottom of these paradoxes has become a recurring theme of this book. My greatest hope is that, after reading it, you will be willing to entertain the idea that people with opinions radically different from yours—even on the most important issues imaginable—are worth having a dialogue with.

Today, same as our ancestors, we live in tribes—although now they are fashionably called filter bubbles.[7] In the past, venturing into another tribe's territory was a dangerous thing to do. Now we can explore filter bubbles outside of our own one without leaving the house. Media can disconnect us, as opinion wars regularly raging on social networks illustrate. But if we start our investigation of other realities from a place of self-awareness and empathy, it should be possible for us to enrich our own worldviews without uncritically accepting other people's beliefs. The next steps can involve having honest yet civil conversations with our opponents, finding ways to reconcile our truths in order to develop a better understanding of the world we live in and looking for solutions that would meet everybody's needs *at the same time*.

Is this ideal a paradox? Perhaps. Perhaps that is why I like it.

When I changed my mind about the Dove body wash ad in 2017, I did not write a quick short post about that transition. As you may recall, my emotions about the situation included embarrassment, sadness, frustration, and fear. At that time, I talked about this experience only with a couple of close friends. In fact, I gradually (almost) stopped sharing my opinions on social media.

I did not write a post about my feelings back then as I did not want to get into online arguments. Yet I spent five years writing *the whole book* on the same topic, knowing that it contains the same controversial ideas! Why? The difference between then and now is that I have learned to use the principle of vulnerability in order to offer my subjective insights with honesty and humility. Instead of offering my opinions in a rush, I took time to investigate them and to produce a detailed argument. For me, this is an essential part of being media literate.

I am now going to invite you to find out more about the reality *I* believe in. Whatever your interpretations of my interpretations will be, I hope the ideas developed on the following pages can be of some help.

NOTES

1. For a discussion about racism in North American popular media, see Behnken and Smithers (2015).

2. If you are not familiar with this controversy: I encourage you to do the same search I did, and look through a couple of articles you will find in order to explore your own reactions.

3. See Ogunyemi (2017).

4. In the scholarly literature on media, this term is always used as a plural: "media are." However, I realized that outside of my field—and outside of academia—people now usually say "media is." The word "media" is indeed a plural form of "medium," but language is changing all the time. I chose to use singular verbs because that's how the majority of people talk today. In other words, the decision to write "media is" and "media does" was determined by my hope that the readership of this book will be broader than media studies scholars and media educators.

5. If you have never heard of this idea or about Brené Brown, I recommend watching her inspiring TED Talk *The Power of Vulnerability*. If you want to dig deeper, read some of her books (Brown, 2010, 2015, 2019).

6. Jung (1953), para. 18.

7. For a detailed exploration of this term and phenomena behind it, see Pariser (2012).

Chapter 1

What Is Media?

Chances are, you know the answer to this question. At least, you *think* you know it. For some of my readers, the response may seem so obvious that they won't feel a need to formulate it. Media is a popular topic, and people both inside and outside of academia have something to say about it. But a spontaneous search for a definition often turns into compiling (or piling up) a list that soon becomes rather confusing and contradictory.

Films, TV shows, ads, books, magazines, radio, video games, and social networks are all popular items that we tend to include in this inventory. If we do not stop there, more specific but seemingly random examples will sprout up in the mix: Superbowl commercials, iPhone, Skype, Microsoft Office, *The Avengers*, Oprah Winfrey, Disney, Google Maps, Mark Zuckerberg, BBC, Donald Trump's Twitter account, Wonder Woman, *How I Met Your Mother*, Fox News Oh my! Most people agree that media is a part of their lives. But what part it is exactly? This remains unclear.

The more we talk about media, the more obvious it becomes that reaching a consensus on what it actually is might be not so easy. Is it channels of communication, like radio and television? Is it communication tools—for example, cameras and computers? Or maybe it is institutions or corporations (think about Comcast and Disney)? Scholars who study this phenomenon often explore specific messages, texts, and representations. Fans of video games and social networks will say that media includes virtual spaces. Toys are also considered a kind of media—did you know about that? According to Cyndy Scheibe and Faith Rogow, money, maps, board games, and clothes (especially those with logos) should be added as well.[1] According to Neil Postman and Marshall McLuhan, media needs to be explored as an environment people exist in, an essential part of their ecosystem.[2]

You have most probably heard an opinion that media is an industry that includes those who work there. But do we consider only big celebrities, or an electrician switching light bulbs at a movie set should be taken into account as well? Many agree that media has something to do with technology, but is it the technology itself, or people who use it, or their practices, or outcomes of these practices, or all of those at once? Perhaps we should just open some dictionaries to find a simple explanation?

Some of those, such as Oxford Learner's and Collins, provide incomplete lists but do not necessarily suggest why something can be added or left out.[3] This does not really bring us closer to a concise unifying definition. Merriam-Webster claims that media is "the system and organizations of communication through which information is spread to a large number of people." Indeed, media is often associated with sending information over distance to a large audience. But what if I Skype with my mom or send a WhatsApp message to somebody in India? What if I am bored at a party and decide to shoot a text to a friend a few feet away from me, because I don't want to say out loud that I want to leave soon?

Over the years of thinking, studying, and teaching about media, I have come to realize one curious thing. When people are asked to think about what media is, most of the time they spontaneously start discussing what they think it *does* (or does not do) to them and others. Do popular films influence people or is it just entertainment? Does using social networks and smartphones shape our identities or our identities dictate how we engage with those spaces and tools? Do we control news or does it controls us? Media has been now systematically studied for about a century (and a topic of an intellectual inquiry even longer than that), yet we still seem to have more questions than answers about it.[4]

In fact, the consensus is so far away that informal conversations often turn into heated debates. Some do not get what the fuss is all about. Why does it matter how made-up characters behave in an imaginary world of a film or a game? Others get emotional, because they see media as a serious problem that needs to be urgently addressed. What about all those violent video games, sexist commercials, addictive social networks? Our children's future may be at stake![5] It does not help that scholars have not reached any consensus either. On the "formal" level of academic literature, opinions are similarly divided.

MEDIA EFFECTS AND ACTIVE AUDIENCES

At the risk of missing out many important details, I suggest placing all these ideas on a continuum running from one extreme powered by the idea that *media influences us in uniform and predictable ways* to the other one, based on the belief that *people can do with media whatever they want*. In the first case, people are seen as mostly passive and media is described as active. In the second case, the situation is reversed. Notably, the first extreme represents not only concerns but also hopes: media can hurt or save us. Yet, it's exactly where the tendency to blame media can be located, which this book talks a lot about. Now let's take a closer look at the two opposing paradigms that I have just named.

Fears about communication technologies have quite a long history. If we assume (as many do) that the first kind of media texts to grace the face of Earth was books, it all started in 1440, when Johannes Gutenberg invented the printing press. Soon after that, printed books were already making some people nervous. Monks, who used to be responsible for reproducing manuscripts, were less than thrilled about the new competition. "He who ceases from zeal for writing because of printing is no true lover of the Scriptures," the abbot Johannes Trithemius warned in the fifteenth century.[6]

One hundred years after the press was invented, Conrad Gessner, known for cataloguing all existing books of the time, complained about their "confusing and harmful abundance." Fast-forward one more hundred years to French scholar and critic Adrien Baillet, who proclaimed: "We have reason to fear that the multitude of books which grows every day . . . will make the following centuries fall into a state as barbarous as that of the centuries that followed the fall of the Roman empire."[7] One has to wonder what these scholarly men would say if they had walked into a book store of today.

(But why start with books? Maybe the first kind of media was tabula rasa—slates covered with wax in the Ancient Rome to write and send messages? Or hieroglyphs on papyruses of the Ancient Egypt? Or engravings on walls of the great pyramids? What if media existed even before that? If we think that it has something to do with technology, perhaps we will need to define what technology is . . . We will return to these questions later in the chapter.)

As some countries were becoming more industrialized, new cultural forms started to emerge with the ever-growing speed. Fears about them were growing as well. Cinema was becoming increasingly popular at the turn of the twentieth century, and some began to worry what the moving images could do to an average person. During the world wars, mass media was used for propaganda by all sides involved, which created concerns about its ability to manipulate large numbers of people.[8]

American media studies grew on the foundation of these fears, and the so-called *media effects* paradigm loomed large at the dawn of the field.[9] Its underlying assumption was that ideas communicated through technology are able to influence people directly and often negatively. In the 1930s, scholars used the hypodermic needle model and the magic bullet theory to claim that media messages can enter the brain of passive audience members, often with devastating results.[10] Nazi propaganda was a popular example and cautionary tale. Meanwhile, some European thinkers created theories claiming that photography and cinema could destroy art.[11]

When television entered the stage, scientists and activists became preoccupied with possible effects of violent content.[12] Using the social learning theory, scholars argued that human beings learn through imitation. If they witness a certain behavior on the screen often enough, they will start repeating it. Bandura's famous experiments with children watching an adult hit a doll and then imitating this behavior were used as evidence.[13] On the foundation of these and similar studies, a troubling argument emerged: consuming certain media may lead to real-world violent acts or to desensitization. As a different take on media effects studies, researchers inspired by cultivation theory counted instances of violent behavior in TV programs and films. They concluded that heavy viewers will see society as more violent than it actually is.[14]

Then in came the Internet, bringing new anxieties. What if browsing the web changes our brains, forcing us to lose our capacity for concentration?[15] What if online social networks actually make us less social and interactions in Internet communities lead to weakening of the "real" connections?[16] As the reach of the World Wide Web was growing, this virtual space became associated with bullying, child abuse, commercialism, and the loss of privacy.

One can see a trend here: the arrival of each new form of media has resulted in a new array of concerns, or even in a moral panic. Some of these fears have been dispelled. Who remembers the craze about subliminal messages—the twenty-fifth frame effect?[17] Yet other suspicions keep many parents awake at night and give activists energy for passionate campaigns.

Here is one example. Within the trend started by Betty Friedan's book *The Feminine Mystique* in the 1960s, scholars analyze media texts to show how they can hurt women.[18] Just to clarify: I think that media representations of gender roles deserve more attention than the potentially hypnotizing effects of the twenty-fifth frame. Indeed, action films have more male than female leading characters, same as books and movies for kids. When female superheroes are fighting villains in most unexpected locales and uncomfortable positions, their hair and make-up seem perfect. Commercials for beauty products overwhelmingly target women, even if those are portrayed as strong and independent. Some concerned consumers draw a cause-and-effect connection between these portrayals and obstacles that women deal with when they try to succeed in politics and business.

It would be wrong to say that the introduction of every new type of media triggers only anxieties. Fears described above often coexist with hopes. For instance, when the World Wide Web became a thing, some people enthusiastically discussed its potential for erasing inequalities. As a famous cartoon published in the *New Yorker* in 1993 put it: "On the Internet, nobody knows you're a dog." Although fears and hopes seem to represent radically different reactions, I see them as two sides of the media effects kind of thinking. We may focus on how "bad" books and films hurt us or pray for "good" alternatives to come and save the world. In both cases, we are talking about *what media can do to us*, about its impact on our lives.

Of course, the definition of "bad" and "good" depends entirely on who the judge is. In 1858, one commentator wrote about a novelty of the time—the transatlantic telegraph: "Superficial, sudden, unsifted . . . . Does it not render the popular mind too fast for the truth? Ten days bring us the mails from Europe. What need is there for the scraps of news in ten minutes?" Yet another article argued about the same innovation: "This binds together by a vital cord all the nations of the earth. It is impossible that old prejudices and hostilities should longer exist, while such an instrument has been created for an exchange of thought between all the nations of the earth."[19]

The media effects perspective has a long history, and it is still influential today. Nevertheless, for the most part of its existence, this view has been balanced out by the opposite approach. Instead of concentrating on the impact that digital devices, magazines, and social networks can have on us, we may choose to wonder *what we can do with their help*.

In the first half of the twentieth century, uses and gratifications theory became the first official step to explore this direction.[20] Scholars within this tradition asked audience members to provide explanations for why they watched television, read books, and went to the cinema. Collected responses included such benefits as being educated, entertained, or informed, connecting to others, and finding relief from stresses of daily life. After this "why" question of media use was asked, it was the matter of time till somebody raised the "how" one.

Earlier in this chapter, I mentioned the European thinkers who were worried that cinema and photography would destroy art. Their fears actually gave way to a less pessimistic—at times even cautiously optimistic—view. As fears about popular culture turned to curiosity, European cultural studies emerged and produced the *active audience* paradigm of thinking about media.[21] The name is pretty self-explanatory: theories within this perspective are based on the assumption that people are not passive victims when they communicate through technology.

According to this standpoint, we can be active media users even when we are not conscious about our choices. Yet paying attention to the "how" question is key. Our backgrounds—family, religion, race, sexuality, education, physical ability, and so on—shape how we engage with media texts, spaces, channels, and tools. At the same time, even more optimistic scholars argued that we should see this engagement in the context of power struggles and inequalities.[22]

According to the ideas about active audience, main claims of the media effects tradition miss the point. For instance, it would be a simplification to argue that people belonging to marginalized social groups can only suffer from media representations. To illustrate this point, Jacqueline Bobo reviewed reactions to the film *The Color Purple* (released in 1985). This period drama tells a story of Celie, a dark-skinned woman abused by her father and then husband. Throughout the movie, Celie slowly gains self-worth and strength to claim happiness. Up till the end of the film, she is portrayed as dependent and submissive, unable (or unwilling?) to fight against her abusers. Nevertheless, many female viewers found the story of Celie's struggles and suffering uplifting. Far from being angered by the representation of the powerless Black woman or simply depressed by this story, they used it as an opportunity to discuss the need to find courage in the unfair world.[23]

Or take the iconic Barbie doll. This toy has been accused of many sins, from promoting unachievable beauty standards to reinforcing heteronormative values. Yet in her book *Barbie's Queer Accessories* Erica Rand describes a surprising variety of ways to interpret the doll that different children and adults have come up with. Even if we think that Mattel's creation epitomizes standards of White able-bodied Western beauty, it is ok as long as people creatively question these values. Rand collected stories about the most imaginative uses that included turning the doll into a punk dyke and a lesbian dildo. It does not matter whether these transformations are a result of social activism or mere playfulness, the author claimed. In all these cases, interpretations envisioned by Mattel give way to a collage of ideas that has little to do with the doll's original purpose.[24]

If everybody interprets and uses media differently, we cannot really talk about any uniform and predictable impact. This is what I personally believe in. However, I do think that we should talk about challenges of using media technology *properly*. For example, if the Internet gives us instantaneous access to infinite information, how do we find what we need without becoming distracted and overwhelmed? If social networks allow us to be civically engaged, how can we contribute to positive social change rather than polarization? Other possible considerations include ethics of online anonymity, strategies of multitasking with multiple devices, or the need to overcome constraints of journalistic practice to deliver news in the least biased manner. I believe that we should practice asking these and similar questions. This would mean making important steps toward developing our media literacy.[25]

Another variation of the active audience perspective is the idea that people cannot be easily divided into active media producers and passive consumers. What if we are all hybrids: *produsers* or *prosumers*?[26] Continuing this logic, such scholars as Henry Jenkins explore what they call the participatory potential of the modern media.[27] They provide compelling examples of people using media tools in innovative ways to become engaged citizens in a democratic society. And when not creating political campaigns, these smart prosumers use materials provided by popular culture to tell stories as part of fandom communities.[28]

Even if we prefer this optimistic perspective, we should not forget to ask whether the potential for participation is distributed equally. Most scholars who favor the active audience paradigm do not believe that there are no problems with communication through technology. Not all potential produsers have equal access to modern tools due to differences in socio-economic status.[29] While some kids have personal computers at home, others need to share slow desktops in their public libraries or schools, where useful content can be blocked by well-meaning administrators. In addition, media technologies come with limitations and hidden values. For instance, it is hard to escape biases of algorithms used to process big data.[30] Last but not least, all the participatory potential can be used to purposefully hurt others, as in the cases of cyberbullying and revenge porn. If we are too optimistic, we will not be fully aware of these nuances and dangers.

Finally, it is not unusual to meet someone who thinks that movies, video games, and TV shows are just entertainment, that computers and cameras are just tools we use to fulfill our needs. These ideas lie on the utmost active audience extreme of the continuum I described in the beginning of this section, where people are seen as totally uninfluenced by media.

I have provided only a glimpse at different opinions, dividing them crudely into two basic paradigms. There are a lot of possible variations between the extremes of "media effects" and "active audiences." Moreover, one person can combine contradictory views. Parents worried about their kids' time with smartphones and video games may consider themselves immune to any negative influence.

This brief overview was meant to further clarify the point I have made in the beginning of the chapter. Most of us do acknowledge that we live in the world where media is something important. However, there is no consensus on how *it* relates to *us*, human beings.

LANGUAGE MATTERS

Although opinions differ, many would agree that media (whatever it is) has some influence on our lives. This is true even for people who believe that audiences and users are not duped or manipulated. For many, media does not need to have predictable and uniform effects for it to remain an issue of inter-est (and potentially of concern). Not every teenager who plays first-person shooter video games will bring dangerous ammunition to their classroom. Does that mean that we can completely ignore the graphic goriness of this type of entertainment? Scholars study media and educators teach about it exactly because they think that our relationship with this phenomenon is not entirely uncomplicated—even though not every person is affected in the same way.

Do we need to understand how websites, apps, and commercials "work" because they can make us (or our kids) violent, sexist, racist, and materialist? Is it because, if we misuse social networks or digital devices, we may hurt others? Or perhaps understanding media will help us spend our time more effectively and benefit from the modern technology instead of being distracted by it? As you could see in the previous section, there is no agreement on what the problem is and how it should be tackled.

And yet, there seems to be an unspoken agreement that the definition of media is something very obvious! Having read numerous books and articles on the subject, I have realized that many authors do not define media before starting to discuss its impact or applications. Most of the attention is spent on inquiries about people's relationship with various media forms. I believe that this is a big mistake. In fact, I think that only if we deeply engage with the question that I used as the title of this chapter we will be able to understand media's problems and properly enjoy its benefits.

There is one important thing that prevents us from truly seeing the nature of media: the language we use to talk about it. Linguists have for a long time debated whether—and if so how—language influences thought. In the beginning of the twentieth century, they came up with a theory of linguistic determinism, which claimed that the language we speak defines the way we think. According to this view, because people from different cultures use different words and grammar structures, they see the world and behave differently. Although the theory of linguistic determinism initially looked intriguing, it was rejected as overly simplistic.[31]

Nevertheless, modern scholars believe that there is at least some connection between how we talk about the world and the way we perceive it. Although language does not define our thinking, it reflects certain beliefs that exist in our culture. Examining the language we speak can help us reveal unspoken assumptions that may secretly influence our lives. This happened, for example, when English-speakers started to wonder why the pronoun "he" is used when people in general are implied.

Harry Weinberg compared language to a human-made map that people use to find their way through the universe. He wrote:

> When our maps do not fit the territory, when we act as if our inferences are factual knowledge, we prepare ourselves for a world that isn't there. If this happens often enough, the inevitable result is frustration and an ever-increasing tendency

to warp the territory to fit our maps. We see what we want to see, and the more we see it, the more likely we are to reinforce this distorted perception, in the familiar circular and spiral feedback pattern.[32]

It is tempting to believe that the world is the way our language describes it. But language is created by people, and it reflects people's flaws.

When we talk about media, we use what can be called the *language of externalization*. To put it simply, our choice of words implies that media exists outside of people. Think about how interested we are in our relationship with media. Whether we are primarily concerned about effects or excited about uses, the key assumption remains the same: media is not us, and we are not media.

Look at the following quote. In their book about representations of race, gender, and class, Bramlett-Solomon and Carstarphen write:

> They [media] tell us what's in and what's out, what's hot and what's not, and they convey what it means to be pretty or ugly, rich or poor, successful or fail-ure, female or male, powerful or powerless, or good or bad. Media define not only our culture but, indeed, most aspects of our lives. The media are a main source of knowledge about our world and, in fact, teach us about the various groups that constitute our society.[33]

Note the use of active verbs. According to the quote above, media is able to tell us stuff, convey ideas, define our lives, and teach us about the world. This wording makes media seem almost like a living entity that has a will of its own.

We externalize media even when we are less preoccupied with its negative influence. We may say that it gives us opportunities, empowers us, or helps us improve society (by teaching people, connecting them, etc.). Alternatively, we can describe it as an object that we act upon: adapt to our needs, modify, negotiate, and interpret. In all these cases, media appears to be *something* that can be used for our benefit, something different from us.[34]

This way of speaking is present even when people say that media is just entertainment, an imaginary world or space created for their enjoyment. The language of externalization appears almost inescapable when we think or talk about this subject.

In all these cases, we refer to media using the third-person pronoun *it* (or *they*, for scholarly writers). Perhaps this is just a figure of speech? In fact, it is not unique. To explain our behavior we may say something like "love/anger/sadness made me act this way." Of course, we know that these feelings are experienced by people; they do not exist outside of us. At the same time, this language reveals an interesting assumption that we may not need to take full responsibility for our actions and choices.

Wait a second: at this point, my readers may recall such items in our list as books, films, magazines, and toys. They definitely are different from us! When we hold a book in our hands, the volume and our body are not merging together. Let me ask you a theoretical question: Will a book be still a book if all of humankind disappears? Will a book be a *book* if it's an object made of paper, glue, and ink lying in the post-apocalyptic dust with nobody to read it forever and ever, till the end of times?

Most people agree that media has something to do with communication and with technology. A book is created as part of a communication process: somebody used its materials (paper, glue, and ink) to encode ideas for others to decipher. But if there is no one to do that, the cycle will be broken. With no one to engage with the author's thoughts, they will simply cease to exist. Ideas live in our heads, after all. The book is just a link between people, and without people it will lose its purpose. It will not be a book anymore.

Same is true for all kinds of messages, texts, and representations. They will not be media if they are not mediating between people engaged in communication. For media to exist, people sharing ideas with each other need to be involved. The points connected through mediation make the act of mediation possible. Same is also true for such tools as cameras, computers, and phones. To be media, they need people to use them for communication. Will a camera still be a camera if somebody uses it to hammer nails? I don't think so.

Other things we considered for our list in the beginning of the chapter included practices (texting), organizations (Google), social networks (Facebook), and all sorts of professions connected to the media industry (journalists, actors, video game designers, maybe even movie set electricians). What all these items have in common is that they involve people. In fact, each item we have mentioned so far is either literally people, or people's practices, or social structures that are made up of people or objects that people use. It turns out that media is *media* only when some technology is facilitating communication between people. This is actually a perfect time to ask ourselves what is this *technology* we are talking about.

Visitors come to El Castillo Cave in Spain to marvel at the humanity's first "selfies"—negative prints of human hands that were created more than 30,000 years ago. To produce them, red hematite was crushed into powder, mixed with water, and then sprayed on the rock using two hollow bones. The purpose of this procedure is still not entirely clear to archeologists. Can it be considered first attempts at art? Was it a part of some ritual? In any case, one thing seems clear: our ancestors were trying to communicate with somebody, to share with the world ideas that existed in their heads. It is unlikely that these creators could imagine the large and puzzled audience their messages would reach in hundreds of their lifetimes.

The mysterious negative handprints may be called first media texts, even though meanings they encapsulated were probably very raw and simple (e.g., "I am alive"). But to call them media, we need to interpret the term "technology" broadly, as a set of human-made tools and practices associated with them. Why should we limit technology to inventions of the industrialized world?

If we broaden our interpretation this way, the division between mediated and non-mediated communication will become blurry. We may say that to communicate directly we rely only on our body. Then what about all the technologies used to change or train our bodies? Don't they count, too? Think about tattoos of ancient tribes and modern subcultures or about the foot binding in China. Tattoos have been known to tell complicated stories. Modifying the shape and size of girls' feet conveyed ideas about their social status, about the beauty standards of the Song dynasty, and about gender roles of the time.

If we take this logic to extreme, language itself could be considered a kind of media technology.[35] It is not something we are born with, but a tool we have to master. Words we use exist outside of us. Yet, same as in the example of the abandoned book, words are only *words* when they are part of human interactions. If words could be caught in a cave as an echo to exist forever, without anybody around to understand their meaning (or at least to try understanding it) they would only be soundwaves bothering bats.

In this book, I argue that the way we talk about media hides a very important assumption, shared by everybody no matter how worried or hopeful they are. This assumption is that media represents something radically different from direct communication. This is suggested by multiple books and articles focusing on the way media has changed our lives. I do not deny the importance of analyzing differences between communication of the past and the modern media forms. At the same time, I advocate for taking a closer look at similarities between the society of the past and the world of today, filled with modern technologies.

I argue that we need to acknowledge that *media is us, people, communicating with each other through technology*. I don't mean to say that this idea is entirely new. Yet, it seems to somehow get lost in our discussions and debates on the subject (not the least because media can be seen as "some other people"). And if we understand technology broadly, we will also have to admit that media has existed for quite a while, probably as long as *Homo sapiens* have been communicating in the uniquely human way.

By pointing out the limitations of the language we use, I do not mean to suggest that it is bad or that those who rely on it are wrong. It's not like we currently have a lot of options. Using new gender pronouns is easier than providing long caveats every time media is mentioned. I myself do not have a different strategy, as you can see if you pay closer attention to my own wording. My goal is not to change the way we speak but to challenge the way we think. By the same token, there is no harm in saying "love makes the world go round." At the same time, it may be useful to become more aware of our choices and responsibilities when strong emotions are involved.

Most importantly, I believe that media is not just *some other* people. It is actually *all of us*, communicating ideas to each other in a million different ways every day, every moment. Media is not neutral because when people interact, they recreate issues that have existed in society since the dawn of the humankind. Some of them were inherited from the animal kingdom outside of our species. We connect and learn, but we also hurt each other and make the same mistakes that our ancestors made numerous times before us. It is important to wonder about media because the problems it is associated with are connected to human nature and social co-existence. But understanding media is not only about acknowledging these problems. It can also help us appreciate the importance of belonging, of passing knowledge from generation to generation, and of maintaining social stability.

FOUNDATIONS OF COMMUNICATION

We tend to think that media is something very different from direct communication—in a sense, much worse. Aren't we surrounded by evidence? Modern technology allows people to store astounding amounts of information on increasingly small devices, to send instant messages to the other side of the globe, and to create fantasy worlds where one can live dozens of lives without leaving the house. Modern technology also provides opportunities for spreading malicious information to large audiences, misusing personal data on a global scale, or distracting people from meaningful relationships with a constant stream of entertainment.

It is true that the age of industrialization introduced a dramatic variety of new cultural practices in a short period of time. I do not suggest discarding the importance of the shock factor that such a rapid change can bring. New forms of communication have plenty of important and unique features that need to be properly understood.[36] However, I believe that behind all this variety and innovations, we can find the same old communication principles that determined how people have been interacting for hundreds of years. And if the modern media appears flawed, we should look for reasons in the nature of humanity and society—not technology.

As you will see, the five principles of communication that I describe below are interconnected. Most importantly, they are all connected to questions that parents, teachers, scholars, activists, and politicians keep asking all over the globe. I argue that these principles determine how we interact with the world around us whether technology is involved or not, and no matter what kind of technology it is.

Principle#1: People need to communicate

We are social creatures and our survival depends on the ability to connect, learn from each other, and collaborate. Communication is essential for human society. It makes society possible. In a circular manner, human interactions are determined by social structures. Communication lies in the heart of tradition and is vital for the existence of culture as the collection of human knowledge, skills, tools, and practices.

Not surprisingly, most of us are always looking for opportunities to stay in touch, discover information, tell stories, and often to be entertained in the process. Communication is in our genes. It has to be, because without it, society as a whole and individuals it is made of would not survive.

Isolation hurts us. This is why solitary confinement is such a tough punishment or why being lost on a boat in the middle of the ocean can make a person lose her mind. Even if we think that we want to "escape the world" for a while—with a favorite book or by binging on a TV show—we are still communicating, only in this case, our interactions with others are mediated. Real hermits who cut themselves off from society in all its manifestations are extremely rare. And it is literally impossible for one to grow up *human* if no other people are involved in the process (stories about children brought up by animals are a case in point).

Communication is beneficial and beautiful, but it is filled with underwater currents that often make us drift away from our best intentions. Since communication is like the air we breathe from the day we are born, we seldom understand how it functions. Needing to interact with other humans all the time does not equal understanding pitfalls we encounter in the process.

Homo sapiens are naturally curious, but wondering where our knowledge is coming from is not an instinct we are born with. This is why people have always loved gossips, centuries ago as well as in the age of tabloids and yellow press. Because we are not very good at distinguishing between different sources, we may trust a person who is in fact lying to our face same as we often trust news without considering its biases, just because reported facts fit our preconceived notions.[37]

People like communication so much that they can easily become carried away.[38] The lack of moderation with some interactions can distract us from such important activities as parenting, working, or studying. We can get addicted to reading books or to reading news online, to maintaining virtual networks or to spending time with friends outside, to sharing tales about co-workers or to following lives of celebrities. We feel the constant need to look for and share information with other human beings, but interactions within our peer networks (whether they happen on- or offline) can make us distracted, confused, and overwhelmed. We can get greedy for new connections but not know how to value and maintain deep relationships. Instead of bonding with peers, we may suffer from pressure and mistreatment or engage in abusive behaviors ourselves.

In order to understand these challenges, we need to see the latest communication forms in the context of this basic human need. In her book *It's Complicated*, danah boyd suggests that young people spend so much time on virtual social networks not because the evil technology corrupts them and not because they do not know how to keep friendships offline. One of the key reasons is that they have fewer opportunities for face-to-face gatherings than their parents did in the past. Of course, as boyd notes, young people who spend a lot of time on social media do make mistakes that may haunt them for years. Persistence of information that we share online creates unique problems that did not exist before. Yet to make sense of media, it is essential to consider our basic desire to communicate with all its complex ramifications, both positive and negative.[39]

Principle#2: By communicating, people create the world around and within them

A friend from France once said to me: "I want to understand what is happening in the United States. I watch news and read newspapers, but I don't entirely trust them. So I want to hear from somebody who currently lives there. You must have a better perspective." My first impulse was to congratulate him on being a careful media consumer. Indeed, many scholars have pointed out for a long time exactly what my friend said. News does not simply report what is going on. News constructs reality.[40]

However, after thinking about my answer for a bit I had to reply:

> You are right, news tell only a part of the story. But I also can only tell you a part of it. It seems that I should know what is going on in the country where I live, but to be honest I really don't. (And if somebody says they know for sure, I would doubt their claim.) Even if you ask me about the city where I reside, I have to admit that I simply cannot witness everything. Most of the things I know about the world, even things happening very close to me, I know through other people. So you can actually only ask me about something very specific that I have seen with my own eyes. Even in this case I will tell you my version of what I saw, my interpretation. It will be mediated through my perception, my unique background and experiences. So I can tell you what *I think* is going on, but it will not necessarily be much more accurate than news, whose objectivity you have very appropriate doubts about.

Media scholars and educators talk a lot about the issue of representation. It is crucial to realize, they say, that media creates reality for us, never showing the world the way it actually is.[41] But we *all* inhabit realities created through communication, and we actively contribute to their existence. Whatever we think surrounds us is actually filtered by our senses and brains. You see the world the way you have learned to see it from other people and tweaked according to your personal characteristics. In this sense, the universe is always represented for us, and we constantly represent it to others in return. Moreover, our identities are produced the same way, including such aspects as age, sexuality, race, physical ability, and gender. These categories themselves are a product of human meaning-making activities.

We are often unaware of these processes. Curiously, we may choose to ignore how they work even if we are offered a chance to see that. Children start playing "pretend" very young, sometimes before the age of two. They pretend to feed their toys with real food or to serve playdough cookies at imaginary tea parties. In these cases, kids clearly understand what is going on and are humored by contrasting the imaginary and the real. Yet in other situations, they can be overwhelmed by their fantasies, for example, when they ask their parents to make sure that no monsters are hiding under the bed. By the same token, grownups themselves often allow their own imagination and imagination of others to have a tangible impact on their lives. We discuss book and film characters as if they existed outside of our heads. We can even fall in love with them or change our habits and appearance to resemble them. It's almost like people ignore these realizations on purpose.

This is perhaps one of the most enigmatic, magical, and overwhelming aspects of communication. As we are creating the world by interacting with others, this world is also creating us. This phenomenon is not new: culture and society have always worked this way. Of course, in the modern times, this relationship may take truly peculiar forms. Professional media makers produce characters and narratives according to what audiences (both real and imaginary) want. These figments take on lives of their own and become part of households around the globe, but not without being tweaked and reimagined in the process. Scholars try to understand these processes by creating their own interpretations of media texts, constructing their own images of professional media producers and global audiences. Reflected in mirrors of millions of minds that are infinitely amplified by the modern technology, the process of presenting, re-presenting, re-re-presenting, and re-re-re-presenting never ends.

Principle#3: Communication happens according to the rules of human perception and cognition

Details of the realities we inhabit are determined by human perception (how we take the world in through our senses) and cognition (how brains process this information). These two are closely related. We communicate with, and about, the world in a certain way because of how our senses function. But information that we get thanks to the senses is filtered through our brains and shaped by them. Our brains, in turn, depend on senses as we get access to the world by touching, smelling, tasting, and hearing it.

Some characteristics of human perception and cognition can be described as flaws. I compare these traits to glitches, because they are limitations of our ability to understand *on the individual level* what's really going on. At the same time, I acknowledge that it would probably be more correct to call them side-effects of otherwise amazing evolutionary accomplishments. We use our eyes to see colors, but we don't have a sense for "seeing" heat as some other animals do. Our ears are not able to process sound waves that bats use for navigation. As for our brains, they have to use dramatic simplification in order to process the complex and chaotic environment. Without this ability, we would be overwhelmed. But because of our tendency for simplification, we often lose important nuances of objects, phenomena, and beings that we encounter. Working in tandem, each individual's senses and brain give her access to the world but not necessarily to the reality that we all long to grasp.[42]

We think in categories, and we expect the world to be rational and predictable. This is why we favor patterns in everything, including narratives. We like hearing familiar stories and seeing archetypical characters because narrative patterns confirm our assumption about the orderliness of the universe. Professional media producers are often accused of not going against people's preconceived notions, of offering them only clichéd representations. The question is, are we really ready for radically new narratives? You'd be surprised to know how difficult it is to challenge age-old archetypes: curiosity about the new coexists with longing for the familiar, even though the novelty of a remix is also welcome.

In the beginning of the twentieth century, influential writer and political commentator Walter Lippman argued that journalists are by definition subjective and that news seldom describes events correctly. But Lippman's goal was not to single out media makers. In fact, he coined the term "stereotype" to highlight how all people's biases shape their perceptions.[43] Today, cognitive psychologists confirm that everybody is indeed biased.[44] Things get even more unexpected when we read about scholarship that describes our morality as based on intuitions rather than on logical reasoning.[45] Other studies argue that our memory can be easily manipulated because it does not work like neat slots where we carefully store important information to be retrieved when we need it.[46] Yet, all of these properties of our senses and brains are not necessarily harmful. They are merely manifestations of elaborate mechanisms that we need to be aware of.

Although all people's brains and senses work in similar ways (with important variations), individuals have distinct worldviews due to personal traits and experiences. All these differences explain the beautiful complexity of society, but they also lead to bitter conflicts that emerge in the process of communication. The bigger the gap of people's experiences, the higher the chance of misunderstanding. One step toward avoiding such conflicts would be to acknowledge that these differences exist. It's good to realize that the way we live our lives is not the only way or not the only *right* way. (This may be challenging because we are usually surrounded by people who think and act similarly to us.) Whenever we share our ideas with others—be it by parenting a child, creating a movie, writing a post on social networks, or gossiping about a party we have attended—we tell things the way we think they are or the way we would like them to be. This does not happen because we are malicious or stupid. It's how human communication works.

Scholars who explore media effects talk about such phenomena as agenda-setting, framing, and priming.[47] They say that media tells us what to pay attention to, what to consider important, and what to think about. But very similar things happen within human interactions that are not mediated by the modern technology. Traits of our perception and cognition determine how we understand what is being communicated to us. For instance, one of the most famous brain "glitches"—confirmation bias—explains our tendency to look for information that confirms what we already believe in, rejecting any contradictions. When we hear something said often enough by people around us, we will be less likely to question it (bandwagon effect). Stereotypes about social groups we belong to determine our ideas about our own abilities (stereotype threat). There is most probably a cognitive bias for every sin that media has been accused of.

To sum it up, challenges of the most recent cultural forms cannot be simply explained by the features of technology. In order to understand them, we need to be aware of how our senses and brains function. For example, algorithms that help us organize big data reflect human imperfections channeled through digital tools. That is why search results or online translations may turn out to be surprisingly racist or sexist.[48] Same as journalists like supporting the myth of journalistic objectivity, some creators of algorithms insist on their creation's neutrality. If Walter Lippmann lived today, he would draw a parallel between the two claims, seeing them both as misleading. But he might also remind us that, instead of focusing on limitations of media professionals, we should see their flaws as part of a bigger picture where everyone's biases (aka evolutionary accomplishments) contribute to the way society functions.

Principle#4: Communication reflects and reinforces power relationships that exist in society

Taking a closer look at communication processes on the individual level, we notice the curious features of our perception and cognition discussed above.

But if we zoom out to see individuals as part of the infinitely complex social system, our focus will have to change. We will need to account for the fact that human beings are constantly struggling to gain or maintain control over limited resources, to achieve their goals despite each other's resistance. Our society is built on battles for power. Some of them are major—between countries, nations, or politicians that determine fates of millions. Others include everyday tug-of-wars between colleagues, friends, siblings, and spouses. In the healthiest relationships, power is fluctuating, fluid. In the abusive ones, it is rigid.

What does communication have to do with these struggles? First, it matters who gets to speak, when, what they can say, and what impact their words are allowed to produce. It matters whose version of reality is accepted as "truly" real and whose opinions remain invisible or devalued. Second, because access to information gives people different opportunities, it determines what each person can do. Having necessary information does not only mean being able to achieve one's goals better. It also means knowing how to set the right goals in the first place. And knowledge is produced through communication.[49]

Same as the previous principles, the fourth one works no matter what kind of technology is involved. Imagine ancient societies where only a few were allowed to important gatherings that discussed the fate of a tribe. Perhaps women or the youngest members were not given an opportunity to express their opinions. In the modern history of the United States, people of African descent were not allowed to vote for a very long time. As a result, they did not have a say in the direction the country was taking. Today, scholars note that the lack of diversity in the influential media industry means that certain points of view are unlikely to produce any serious ripple effect.[50] It is believed that people with more power are the ones to shape everybody's perceptions of the world, because they decide how to represent it for others—in news, books, films, commercials, and so on.

It is also believed that these influencers have power because their social characteristics—gender, race, physical ability, and so on—allow them to have better access to important information. Knowledge is power, as they say.[51] In the past, this could equal knowing a path to a hidden treasure or to a source of drinking water. It could mean being informed of where the enemy is hiding and when they are planning to attack. In the modern world, knowledge that gives power may come in the form of being aware of how to properly prepare for a standardized test that grants access to better education and career opportunities. "Digital divide" is a term used to describe another form of power imbalance: differences in access to information distributed through the modern technology.[52] In simple words, not everybody owns a personal computer or a smartphone. Even those who own them do not necessarily know how to look for information that would benefit them or how to add their voices to the global conversation on important social issues.

The concept of power seems obvious, but it has a number of definitions and interpretations. Civil rights movements of the twentieth century introduced the vision of power as attached to certain traits, such as masculinity, light skin, heterosexuality, and physical ability.[53] A major revelation was that some social groups are allowed to speak for others, and that it's not right. Scholars also discovered that powerful voices are amplified by technology. This realization led to criticism of some media representations described as insufficient and of professional media producers called insensitive and biased.

However, there is another interpretation of power: it can be seen as fluid, not belonging to specific individuals and groups but given to them by society through processes of communication.[54] This interpretation does not have to negate the first one, yet their coexistence creates a paradox that has to be resolved. Trying to understand how communication works on a deeper level, we will notice that the struggle for power happens not only between individuals belonging to different social groups. It also takes place between every individual and the social system as a whole, which imposes on each one of us certain ways of seeing the world, being in it, and communicating about it.

Principle#5: People influence each other through communication

Can media influence the way we live our lives? If we see media as people communicating with each other, the answer becomes obvious. Yes, it can and it certainly does.

From the day we are born, we are socialized—become part of society—through communication. We learn from others how to understand the world and ourselves. We develop our individual versions of reality that depend on people around as much as on shared properties of our brains and unique physical characteristics. Do people influence each other? Of course, this is what socialization is all about! We are influenced by those who we meet in person and by those who live on the other side of the globe; those who will never know about our individual existence, and those long gone. In response, we also influence other people over time and space. Each one of us does it. Most of the influences we experience and produce are mediated. So you can say that media influences people in a sense that people influence each other.

Can we hurt each other in the process of communication? We certainly can and we do so all the time. In the modern society, media—understood through the language of externalization—has become the usual suspect. We blame it for a variety of issues, including violence, consumerism, and political polarization.[55] But the existence and persistence of the problems media has been blamed for can be understood differently. They may be so difficult to eliminate exactly because *media is us* and because we are constantly shaping each other's lives, sometimes in unfortunate ways.

Human beings can uplift, give hope, inform, and entertain. They can also masterfully use each other's weaknesses, manipulate, deceive, offend, and confuse. The harm can be done on purpose or through the lack of awareness. Without realizing it, I can say something that will make you very sad. I can easily forget that you see a situation differently and tell only my version of the story, making it seem like the common truth. I can hide from you something that I know in order to make you act in a way that will benefit me. I can persuade you that acting this way is in your best interest. Notice, that all of these things can be done no matter what kind of technology people use.

The tendency to *mis*inform each other stems from our own lack of knowledge about what is going on, combined with the firm belief that we possess this knowledge after all. As a poet Alexander Pope famously wrote, "To err is human." Of course, sometimes we *dis*inform each other on purpose.[56] Disinformation has existed since our distant ancestors started to communicate in the uniquely human ways. Or probably even earlier, as some animals are also known to confuse each other, for example, regarding the location of hidden food.[57] Around 2016, the world became obsessed with the notion of fake news.[58] Media channels and professionals have been accused of promoting "alternative facts" and damaging the modern democracy. But fake news is nothing new. Ask squirrels as they are diligently creating a stash for a snack that is not there.[59]

Of course, to understand how people influence each other in the modern society we should take characteristics of the modern technology into account. Fake news can spread through social networks like fire, which is different from how misinformation and disinformation functioned before the age of the Internet. Yet, we also should not forget that fake news do not emerge simply because of media technology. Their impact can be explained by referring to people's biases as much as to the properties of the World Wide Web.

All these visible and invisible influences should be seen in the context of the conversation about power that I briefly introduced above. Because people influence each other, power relationships may be more complex than we think. It is important to acknowledge that some have more opportunities to exercise their control over others *under certain circumstances*. Further exploring how communication functions, we may discover that these opportunities are rooted in ideas that people with different levels of privilege reproduce through their everyday actions. This controversial claim will be explored in the following chapters of the current book.

If we understand technology broadly, it is not as easy to divide forms of communication into mediated and non-mediated ones. In the old days, people shared ideas through the spoken and written word, but also by modifying their bodies, wearing certain clothes, and surrounding themselves with objects to signify a certain status. In the modern world . . . we do the same. Our interactions may seem radically different because today we are surrounded by phones, computers, and other digital devices. Our ancestors did not have a variety of screens to look at, but they still found multiple ways to connect, learn, and tell their truths. They invented stories and listened to tales told by others, whether they believed them to be true or not. Through communication, they shaped each other's lives, often in ways that fell within the gray area, as it was impossible to say whether they were good or bad. This has not changed.

Because communication comes to us so naturally, we seldom think about its underlying challenges, instead focusing on the recent changes, because they are more visible. As a result, we do not notice how our senses and brains affect the way we create the world around us as we are interacting with each other. We are concerned about other people's actions and their impact on our lives, but seldom consider how *we* shape the world that others inhabit. We lack this awareness not because we are stupid. Society is infinitely complex, and we are part of it. It is not easy to study ourselves.

At this point, I expect (indeed, hope) that my readers have more questions than answers. You might still not be persuaded that communication through modern technology is similar to human interactions prior to the industrial age. Even if we agree that media is people, how about all the differences between audiences and professional media producers? After all, not everybody works in the media industry. Those who do, seem to have more power to shape the public opinion than average Janes and Joes staring at their screens. Does the argument about fluidity of power that I hinted at mean that we are all equally to blame for society's deficiencies? For some, this may sound like an insult! In the following chapters, I am going to gradually address these important questions and concerns.

NOTES

1. Scheibe and Rogow (2012).

2. These scholars introduced a field known as media ecology. See McLuhan (1964) and Postman (1985).

3. According to Oxford Learner's Dictionaries, media is "the main ways that large numbers of people receive information and entertainment, that is television, radio, newspapers, and the Internet." According to Collins, "You can refer to television, radio, newspapers, and magazines as the media."

4. Here are some examples of scholarly work on the role of the modern media in people's lives. Walter Benjamin wrote about the potential impact of mass media in

his seminal essay *The Work of Art in the Age of Mechanical Reproduction* back in the 1930s. In the beginning of the twentieth century, Harold Lasswell contributed to the emerging media studies as part of the U.S.-based Institute for Propaganda Analysis (see Lasswell et al., 1935). In the first half of the twentieth century, Paul Lazarsfeld applied psychological and statistical approaches to investigate how media impacts political opinions (see Lazarsfeld et al., 1944).

5. For a thought-provoking discussion about why a variety of social problems have been associated with media, see Sternheimer (2013).

6. This quote was reprinted in Brann (1981), p. 158.

7. Both quotes were taken from Blair (2003), p. 11.

8. To better understand the emergence of propaganda studies, see Cole (1996).

9. History and the current state of media effects scholarship was comprehensively described by Bryant, Thompson and Finklea (2012), Davis and Wartella (1996), as well as Lowery and DeFleur (1983).

10. Berlo (1960), Schramm (1973).

11. These were concerns expressed by scholars within the influential Frankfurt School. See Adorno and Horkheimer (2002[1947]).

12. Research on media violence is far from uncomplicated. Although many respectable scholars argue that effects of violent media content are a serious cause for concern, others claim that such fears are exaggerated. For one perspective on the subject that I personally find compelling, see Gauntlett (2005).

13. Bandura (1962).

14. This effect came to be known as the "mean world syndrome." For a critical analysis of cultivation theory, see Potter (2014).

15. Carr (2010).

16. Turkle (2017).

17. It is believed that the human brain cannot distinguish between more than 24 frames per second. (The actual number of frames the brain registers may not be as precise as this.) The concern about the twenty-fifth frame came from the idea that if we are shown an additional frame for a mere 1/25 second, the image it contains can directly affect the subconscious part of our mind. For example, if we are watching a documentary about whales with some 1/25 second frames containing images of Coca-Cola bottles embedded here and there, we will suddenly experience an urge to consume this drink that we won't be able to explain.

18. See Friedan (2001[1963]). For an overview of feminist media studies, see Harvey (2019). For a discussion on scholarship of gender in the media, see Gill (2007).

19. These quotes can be found in Lafrance (2014), in paragraph 3 and Briggs (2012[1923]) on page 22, respectively.

20. Blumler and Katz (1974).

21. The Centre for Contemporary Cultural Studies, which existed between 1964 and 2002 in Birmingham, UK, played an essential role in the development of the active audience approach. For more information, see Turner (2002).

22. One of the most famous scholars of the Centre for Contemporary Cultural Studies was Stuart Hall. His encoding/decoding theory describes how different

interpretations of media texts emerge and explains their relationship to interpretations intended by media producers. See Hall (2003[1980]).

23. Bobo (2002).

24. Rand (1995).

25. Media literacy is understood as a set of skills that can help people navigate the media-saturated world (Hobbs, 2021). To learn about the history of this field, see the essay *The Past, Present, and Future of Media Literacy Education* by Renee Hobbs and Amy Jensen (2009). It is worth mentioning that media literacy approaches can be also placed on the continuum running from "what media does to us" to "what we do with media," with many nuances in the middle. Educational paradigms corresponding to these extremes are known as "protectionism" and "empowerment," although it would be wrong to see them as mutually exclusive (Friesem & Friesem, 2019).

26. The term "produser" was introduced by Axel Bruns in his book *Blogs, Wikipedia, Second Life and Beyond* (2008). The concept of "prosumer" was coined by Alvin Toffler (1980).

27. Jenkins (2006).

28. Jenkins (1992).

29. These inequalities are known as "digital divides." See Compaine (2001).

30. Noble (2018) discusses how biases against women of color can be embedded in search engine results and algorithms.

31. According to linguistic determinism, language determines thought and culture in which it is spoken. A more moderate version of this idea is that language influences thought but does not determine it. To learn more about these perspectives, see Hickmann (2000).

32. Weinberg (1959), p. 29.

33. Bramlett-Solomon and Carstarphen (2014), p. 3.

34. It is not surprising then, that the term "media use" is so popular in discussions about the role of the modern technology in our lives. Some believe that media use is on the rise, as it now includes watching TV, browsing the web, listening to car radio, texting to our friends, and much more. They say that media use is difficult to calculate because all of us are multitasking (e.g., reading news on the smartphone while listening to iTunes). And of course, too much of it can be a problem.

35. I must thank my friend Geoffrey Grossman for sharing this idea with me in a personal conversation. But we were not the only ones to think about this. For example, Jeff Lewis in his book *Media, Culture, and Human Violence* (2016) writes: "In a very real sense, spoken language (speech) represents the first major communication technology and a system that we might call 'media'" (p. 7).

36. For instance, danah boyd (2010) describes four properties of online interactions: persistence (all content is archived), searchability (content can be accessed through search), replicability (content can be replicated), and scalability (content has potentially great visibility). This makes online communication clearly different from interactions happening offline.

37. In his book *The Righteous Mind*, Haidt (2012) argues that our brains are not wired to find the objective truth, but to confirm our preconceived notions.

38. By the same token, the fact that we need to eat does not mean that we naturally have healthy eating habits.

39. boyd (2015).

40. Higdon (2020), Masterman (1985).

41. For example, Scheibe and Rogow (2012).

42. To illustrate how this process works, neuroscientist Edward H. Adelson invented the so-called Checkershadow Illusion. When we look at the image created by Adelson, we perceive two specific squares on the checkerboard (marked A and B) to be of different colors (A is black and B is white), while they are actually of the same color. You can explore this illusion if you print out the image, cut out the two squares in question and put them next to each other (the same can be done on your computer in Photoshop or Print). Adelson explained: "As with many so-called illusions, this effect really demonstrates the success rather than the failure of the visual system. The visual system is not very good at being a physical light meter, but that is not its purpose. The important task is to break the image information down into meaningful components, and thereby perceive the nature of the objects in view" (Adelson, 1995). This serves as great examples of how limitations or our perception and cognition actually make a lot of sense from the evolutionary point of view.

43. Lippman (1922).

44. Ariely (2010), Banaji and Greenwald (2013), McRaney (2012).

45. Haidt (2012).

46. Loftus and Ketcham (2013), McRaney (2012).

47. Bryant, Thompson, and Finklea (2012).

48. Bruns (2019), Noble (2018).

49. I want to briefly acknowledge that important nuances exist between terms "information" and "knowledge," as well a "wisdom," "data," and "truth."

50. Bramlett-Solomon and Carstarphen (2014).

51. This old wisdom was reinterpreted by Michel Foucault, who introduced the concept of "power-knowledge"(1998[1976]).

52. Media literacy education is seen as offering important strategies and tools for tackling some of these challenges (see Jenkins et al., 2009).

53. The idea that society is divided into groups with unequal access to power comes from Karl Marx's analysis of power as attached to different classes. Although Marx focused on economic relationships, scholars and activists that came after him expanded his ideas about powerful and powerless groups (aka oppressors and oppressed) to emphasize other characteristics—notably, gender and skin color.

54. Foucault (1998[1976]).

55. Bruns (2019), Sternheimer (2013).

56. The difference between disinformation and misinformation is that the first one is considered to be intentional, while the second one is not.

57. This phenomenon is described by de Waal (2009) on pages 97–99 of his book *The Age of Empathy*.

58. Higdon (2020).

59. Steele et al. (2008).

Chapter 2

Imperfect Meaning-Makers

What happens if we modify the way we think about media and see it as part of our own everyday communication practices, not as something outside of us? If we don't get distracted by the fascinating novelty of the modern technology and instead explore the underlying principles hidden in the plain sight? This might mean accepting a new worldview that is at the same time liberating and frightening. We don't have to be afraid of the evil media that can ruin our lives. *We* are what brings it to existence, so we should be able to control it. But this also means discovering new responsibilities: to understand how we create the world around and within ourselves by interacting with each other, to acknowledge properties of our senses and brains, to think of ways to challenge society's problems by changing how *we* communicate.

I do not suggest that there is no difference whatsoever between meeting friends face-to-face and sharing pictures on social networks, between lying to one person and lying to an audience of millions, or between reading a book and opening Google Search. It is important to know how communication happens when the modern technology is involved: possibilities of anonymity, persistence of the digital footprint, black box of algorithms. At the same time, we should consider the new cultural forms in the context of basic communication principles that can be explained by referring to the human nature. As you will see, these same principles also define traits of our society, making it possible.

Communication is such an essential part of being human that, as the saying goes, we cannot not communicate. Whatever people do, they "tell" something to others around them. Or whatever they *don't do*! If I stand aside while everybody else on my team is working, I show my attitude about the activity that I decided not to be a part of, and about the people involved. If I don't respond to an email with a thank you note, this is likely to say something about me to the person on the other side of the electronic exchange. Simply by "just living my life," I reveal to others my values, beliefs, and assumptions. All our actions and non-actions become messages to be interpreted and used for defining further interactions.[1]

Communication is often practically invisible to us in its common-sense-ness, yet its outcomes are hard to miss. On the largest scale possible, it keeps together the fabric of our society and allows human culture to exist. Because we share information with others, we can learn from experiences of our ancestors and contemporaries. It saves a lot of time not to invent the wheel again and again. Thanks to our ability to share our intentions with others, we can set and achieve common goals through the wonders of collabora-tion.[2] Finally, it's great to articulate comforting explanations when things go wrong, to relax by listening to stories, and to heal by laughing together.

Yet, communication is not only benign: it also plays a major role in maintaining a variety of social problems: prejudice, discrimination, and inequalities. Why? Simply put, human beings are not perfect.[3] Our imperfections are revealed through communication and shape the way we interact. It is perhaps because of this vicious circle, coupled with the invisibility of these everyday processes, that society's flaws are so difficult to eliminate. To make things even more complicated, human imperfections are intrinsically connected with our greatest evolutionary strengths. Historically, it has been helpful to divide everybody into "us" and "them" because this way we knew whom to trust. But at the same time this has meant perceiving everybody through differences instead of looking for traits in common. The lack of trust can protect us, yet it can also make us paranoid and lonely.

Birds and bees seem to communicate as well, buzzing and chirping cheerfully as days go by. So what it is about human interactions that makes them so special? Why haven't squirrels produced unique civilizations that have survived through centuries? The answer lies in our tendency to create, share, and look for meanings everywhere we go. I am talking about communication *through symbols*.[4]

WHAT DO YOU MEAN?

In November 2010, when Barbara Holmes and Tom Williams moved into a new house in Sacramento, California, many people were shocked. They stopped by and questioned the couple: "Why would you do it? I would never." The house was in bad condition, it's true. It needed some major renovations. But it looked nice, and for a building this size, it was really cheap. So what was the problem? Why was the so-called "1426 F street" affordable yet still available after more than a decade of being empty?

The reason was simple: it used to be a dwelling of a serial killer, and the site of at least nine murders. In this location, an inconspicuous Dorothea Puente ran a boarding house where she preyed on elderly and mentally disabled boarders in order to cash their Social Security checks. In 1988, seven bodies were unearthed in the yard and Dorothea Puente went to jail.

Barbara Holmes and Tom Williams did not find this story a good enough reason not to seal the deal. For them, it was just a nice historic home in need of some reparations. (The fact that it was listed as "historic" was why it was not demolished after the gruesome crimes had been uncovered.) They liked the challenge and were not too bothered by the neighbors' disbelief. In fact, Tom exercised his quirky sense of humor by adorning the house and its fence with plates that said, among other things, "Keep out from under the grass!" and "It was that awful, awful woman that did it! Don't blame me!" signed "The House." Not that Tom and Barbara thought that what had happened in the "1426 F street" was a laughing matter or that Puente's victims should be forgotten. The new owners had another idea in mind: to show the Sacramento community that the house was innocent.[5]

This was a valuable lesson, indeed. It revealed something very important. People think of themselves a meaning-seekers, working hard to understand the world. But the meanings they "find" are actually produced by their brains, and this is where they reside. With a certain mental effort, even the most "obvious" and "natural" of these associations can be undermined. But until their human-made nature is brought to the surface, they may have a surprising power over us.

We are avid communicators from the very beginning of our lives. Babies use an astounding variety of facial expressions, body movements, and noises produced by vocal cords trying to give grown-ups an idea of how they feel or what they want. Our first communicative acts border on instincts and reflexes, similar to those that form the basis of interactions between animals.

A deer informs its mates about danger by flaring or flicking its tail. A whale sings under the surface of the ocean during the mating season or to mourn the loss of a loved one. A dog rolls on its back in submission or as a part of a game. Animals, including insects, communicate not only through sound and sight but also through touch, smell, and taste. Some of these practices appear to be quite sophisticated. They convey messages not only over space but also over time: think of a cat marking its territory with a smelly secretion that can be "read" by neighborhood felines later.

Yet, as human babies grow and their brains mature, communication practices they engage in surpass in their complexity any interactions that take place in the rest of the animal kingdom. And it is thanks to this uniqueness that we become part of society, which is dramatically different from even the largest and most well-organized packs, flocks, and swarms.

Human communication is so special because, unlike animals, we share information by creating and interpreting symbols. I am not just talking about flags and road signs. In sociology, symbols are objects (broadly defined) that represent something beyond themselves. Basically, any aspect of our reality can be a symbol for us as our mind connects it to a variety of ideas that have little to do with physical characteristics.[6]

What do I mean when I say that symbols are objects "broadly defined"? What kind of "aspects of our reality" can they be? Symbols include actual physical objects, but also people, natural phenomena, cultural practices, facial expressions, body movements, sensations, feelings, and words. Tornado can make us think of destruction and death or of the terrifying beauty of nature. Smoking may be associated with being sick or with being cool. A police officer can be seen as a peacekeeper or as a racially biased perpetrator of violence. It all depends on how you look at it.

Words are symbols because their meanings usually have nothing to do with the physical (written or spoken) form. A white dove is a symbol because in certain cultures it represents purity and hope, although there is nothing in the bird itself that would make such associations natural. In fact, some would say that pigeons are quite dirty and annoying, regardless of their color. In case of the "1426 F street," there was nothing in the house itself that made it different from other residences in the area, besides associations that existed only in people's heads. It is the artificial nature of these associations that Barbara and Tom were trying to expose by mocking people's fears and superstitions (but not the seriousness of the crimes).

Some symbols seem to exist separately from each other and some form part of a system: for example, words make up language. Symbols can be verbal and nonverbal, tangible and intangible. Basically, anything we perceive through our senses and brains in the world around us or inside us can be a symbol.

Physical objects surrounding us in our everyday lives are seemingly the easiest symbols to discuss. However, ideas associated with even the simplest things are often more complicated than we expect. Take, for example, an armchair, which some of my readers might be sitting in as they are going through these words. First of all, imagine a person who comes from a culture where armchairs (or anything like it) do not exist. As bizarre as it may seem, this person won't know an armchair's purpose. They will lack awareness of all the associations that an armchair evokes in your brain. Second, think of different layers of meanings attached to different kinds of armchairs. You can find a definition of this object in a dictionary. Yet, this explanation will only scratch the surface of what it can be for different people: a historian, a collector, a designer, a factory worker, an owner of a furniture store, an old person who can't walk, a burglar, a dentist's patient, an exiled king, and so on.

We even understand ourselves through meanings. We define ourselves according to our gender, race, age, sexuality, physical ability, religious beliefs, and many other culturally created characteristics. Some say that we see ourselves through other people's eyes. But can we really do that? Probably not. In fact, this perception is what *we think* others think of us, and it is based on a host of meanings that have a powerful influence on our lives.[7]

For something to be a symbol it needs to mean something to us, or at least we should be trying to understand its meaning. If you feel a strange aching in your body, you might not know what it is but you will work hard to give it a name in order to decide what it implies. You might get it wrong, even when doctors are involved. But the most important point is that you will look for a meaning of this sensation, and then act according to what you discover. Same is true for any feelings and emotions. You don't need to have a word for them to know that you are experiencing something. But what is it exactly? Love or hate? Excitement or fear? That's up to you to decide.[8]

All aspects of our reality have shared meanings that range from associations that a large number of people have, to ideas that make sense within local cultures and communities, to individual memories connected to unique experiences. To make matters more complicated, we can access all these various meanings through different senses. In other words, it's not only about what we see but also what we touch, taste, hear, and smell.

The whole first volume of the famous novel *In Search of Lost Time* by Marcel Proust is built around a memory evoked when the narrator tastes a madeleine cake dipped in tea. This thought about the past branches out into stories about his childhood, the complicated relationship with his mother, people who influenced his intellectual and emotional growth, his first love, and much, much more. You can think about walking into the dentist's office and immediately being overwhelmed with feelings (probably, not the most pleasant ones) because of smells that linger in this environment. As for the touch, we can imagine a person having a strong reaction to a certain tactile sensation, because he suffers from the post-traumatic stress disorder. A good friend of mine was once eating a delicious soup. In the process, she was told that it was actually made of a squirrel. As if by magic, the soup literally changed its taste *for her* and became unsavory. (A parallel example, although more dramatic and gruesome, can be found in the film *Soylent Green*.) Our reality can change in seconds, in ways big and small, just because meanings we are dealing with have shifted.

Symbols influence what we (think we) can do. Being afraid to conform to a stereotype about our social group, we might end up conforming to it after all. Sociologists call such self-fulfilling prophecy "stereotype threat."[9] For example, studies show that some women perform badly on math tests because they think that their gender makes them bad at math. This rule might work also when no social group is involved. If someone undermined your self-esteem by saying that you are a lousy dancer, you might in fact dance horribly just because you think you do. But if this someone praises you instead, you might show wonders on the dance floor.

Although all these ideas exist in our heads, they shape our feeling, attitudes, and actions. They also determine other people's feelings, attitudes, and actions toward us! When a group of people shares meanings that structure their activities and define common goals, this phenomenon can be called a social institution. This complicated term stands for things like family, religion, education, justice system, and media industry. Social institutions exist thanks to meanings we assign not only to physical objects but also to each other, to different actions we perform and to roles we play. The power of meanings is often so strong and their origins are so obscure that it feels like they exist outside of people. They become "just the way things are."

For example, within the justice system a person called "judge" has a specific role which determines what she is supposed to do. She performs predefined actions, uses certain tools (including special garments and a gavel) and interacts with other people in particular ways. It appears that meanings of a judge are not determined by an individual who assumes this role or by people around him. But it is exactly through people's repeated actions that these ideas acquire the power over them. The paradox of meaning-making is that while we can change shared associations, we also have to obey them in order to feel part of the predictable social order.

Anthropologists know well that symbols guiding us are embedded in the environment we create around ourselves. As my sister- and bother-in-law put it while summarizing research about hunter-gatherer societies, "[t]he design of the house, its orientation, the location of objects in it and the points of views and social interactions it allows are direct and indirect statements about proper conduct, which dictate patterns of behaviour and meanings."[10] In fact, same can be said about many other spaces structured around certain social institutions. In terms of education, a school classroom or a university auditorium dictate what can happen there. This space determines roles of different participants as well as power relations between them. Same is true for the place where you work, public spaces you visit throughout the day, and even different areas of your own house.

For a modern person, same as for hunter-gatherers of the past, roles and rules imposed by their environment are taken for granted and non-transparent. The paradox is that *we*, together with people around us, create ideas that shape our lives, but we are seldom aware of that because we externalize these meanings. Symbols have power over us because we let them to, because we accept them as the way things should be. Even when we discover that not everybody sees the world the way we do, we still keep insisting on some naturally occurring objectivity. We point at our living environment as an evidence that unchanging meanings do exist. And the circle continues.

I want to underline the fact that meanings embedded in different aspects of our realities are not absolute and natural. At the same time, I do not want to imply that these meanings are so easy to change. This is one of the essential paradoxes of being human. All of us are beneficiaries and captives of meanings we have accepted, or that have been imposed on us. We can change them, we sometimes try, and we even succeed, but in ways that reinforce some ideas while shifting others. The webs of meanings human beings have created (as Clifford Geertz would put it) are just too complicated to disentangle.[11]

This is a crucial thing to understand. While meanings may seem random and they do vary greatly, it would be wrong to dismiss them. Indeed, it can be disrespectful or even cruel to suggest that something that is important for another person but not for *you* is indeed a trifle (think about violating a sacred space.) If a meaning has a power over a person, this power should not be underestimated. Though it is theoretically possible to undermine and modify even the deepest values and beliefs, one should not force this change on another human being.

THE WORLDS WE LIVE IN

Who wouldn't argue that a coherent reality exists and that we can access it using our senses and brains, unless they are impaired? And yet, in the twentieth century, some scholars started to seriously doubt that. Their doubts were actually not new, but they were suddenly taken to extremes not only by philosophers (who have always been known for their strange speculations) but even by some sociologists and psychologists.[12] Approaching the issue from different perspectives, some of these thinkers concluded that people might actually live in different realities that exist in their own heads. This is not to say that there is no objective world but rather that each individual only has access to its subjective aspects. We don't see things as they are, we see them as *we* are.[13]

A well-known Indian tale about three blind men and an elephant comes to mind. According to the story, after touching the animal, each man came to a very different conclusion about it. They were all right, of course, but they were also wrong because every person argued that he was the only one who had found the truth. To understand what the elephant is, they would have needed to acknowledge the validity of each other's experiences and to combine them, however contradictory those seemed to be.

The reality each one of us inhabits is, indeed, coherent but mostly because we work hard to keep it this way. We dismiss or rationalize inconsistencies, focusing on patterns that make predictions and explanations easier. We produce new information based on what we already know. We "discover" meanings. And if things refuse to make sense, we feel deeply troubled. That's why such words as "nonsense" and "meaningless" as well as the expression "It does not make sense!" bear overtly negative connotations.

In his novel *Les Misérables*, Victor Hugo follows a character named Javert, who—first as a prison guard, and then as a police inspector—has been obsessed with his goal to catch the protagonist Jean Valjean. At the end of the novel, Javert finally gets close to fulfilling his life's mission. But by observing Jean Valjean taking care of a wounded child, Javert suddenly discovers a fatal inconsistency in the meanings he has been operating with all along. Jean Valjean is a criminal who must be punished by law, but he is also a good person who deserves forgiveness. Unable to deal with his moral contradiction, Javert drowns himself in the river Seine. This is an extreme example, of course, but mostly because we successfully ignore the existence of realities that put our own universal order in question.

Imagine a group of people who have come together for a party. They occupy the same space: a house, the city where this house is located, and more broadly—the same country, continent, planet, universe. They also exist in the same time, let's say 6:30 pm, when the party is supposed to begin. The gathered individuals share at least one language, the greatest human-made symbolic system of all, which seems to serve as a further proof that they live in exactly the same reality. So when Susan says to Laura: "I love your dress," Laura understands perfectly well which dress Susan is talking about. When Bill asks Peter "Could you bring me some beer?" he expects—not without a good reason—to get a bottle of beer and not a glass of milk. And if Carolyne asks Mark what time it is, he will look at his watch or produce his smartphone to give a quick answer.

This shared reality is not an illusion. Yet each of the people present at the party experiences her or his own *version* of it, all of them by definition incomplete.

Susan and Bill own the house. For them, it is filled with memories of their youth, their children growing up, and much more. They look at an old armchair and see what nobody else notices: marks of their dog's teeth on its legs. The dog was chewing them when it was a puppy, making Susan and Bill very annoyed at the time because the armchair was brand-new, a wedding gift from Bill's mother. That was many years ago, and the dog since passed away. Now the marks of its teeth produce bittersweet nostalgia. All these memories and feelings are invisible to the guests, for whom it's "just a chair."

Mark has been recently diagnosed with cancer, so he keeps thinking about that. Whatever he sees is colored by his fear of death. For Mark, the party is going too slow, he is stressed and tired. Carolyne is happy because her daughter is coming for a visit tomorrow. This shapes her perception of time much more than whatever the clock says. Carolyne notices a vase that she had given to Susan for her last birthday and that makes her even happier. But Laura thinks the vase is ugly. She went to an art school where teachers told her that this sort of decorations is kitschy.

This is just a tip of the iceberg. We did not even start talking about these people's values and beliefs, and we can't possibly detail all the life experiences that create their current perception of "here and now." Assuming this is the United States, the guests might be middle or upper-class, republicans or democrats, Catholics or atheists, pro or against guns, pro or against abortion, born in the country where the party is taking place or immigrants, straight, gay, or bisexual, single or in a relationship, with children or without, academics, lawyers, politicians, police officers, or accountants, in love or considering a divorce, abused as kids or perpetrators of abuse, allergic to cats or dust, afraid of spiders or snakes, worried about being fired or considering firing an employee, experiencing a toothache or a headache, hating their recent haircut or proud to show off a new outfit, and so forth.

We can say that Susan, Laura, Bill, Peter, Carolyne, and Mark live in different realities not in some sci-fi sense but because of the different meanings they have in their heads. When the meanings overlap, it feels like these people occupy the same time and space. If asked to name objects on a kitchen table, they will produce a similar list. The common language will fool us because it will hide nuances of associations, emphasizing instances of their intersection. But if we ask the gathering to talk about more complicated topics (presidential elections or gun laws), it may well turn out that there is no consensus, although they will still be using the same words. Instances when meanings dramatically diverge (if Bill thinks that God exists, but Peter thinks that she doesn't) remind us that we have on our hands a bunch of "blind men" studiously touching a rather indifferent "elephant," for the universe does not seem to care much what we think about it.

Symbols divide us because they represent different things for different people, yet they also unite us thanks to their shared meanings. Language helps a lot as it brings common associations to the surface. Thanks to language, we understand each other (well, at least we think we do). We can coordinate our actions, which allow us to create things together: to build ships, castles, temples, and whole civilizations. We can pass along our knowledge, even though in the process it often gets reinterpreted. We can exist as society however conflicted it is.

As much as we need to admit the existence of multiple realities that different people inhabit, we should not underestimate the importance of intersections. Shared meanings have as much power over us as the individual ones. It is important to acknowledge that we are part of numerous overlapping *meaning communities*, from a circle of friends with similar memories to nations that share territory and history. Beliefs that exist within these communities unite them and simultaneously separate them from other groups: think about political or religious affiliations. Being a part of a group creates a pleasant feeling of belonging, but it also means the pressure to fit in, which we do by accepting and reinforcing associations that already exist within different communities.

Finally, there are some meanings so powerful and deep that they travel across borders of distinct cultures, even if those are separated by *meaning wars*. Scholars sometimes call these shared assumptions "dominant ideologies."[14] They are usually very simple—perhaps, that's exactly why they can unite so many people at once. For example, the color white in the European tradition is often associated with something positive (purity, wisdom, kindness) and contrasted with black, which is perceived as negative (sin, death, dirt). In comparison, in some Asian countries white is associated with mourning, so this color would not be a good choice for a wedding. Of course, even dominant meanings are not absolute. They can be more or less prominent depending on the context: a little black dress at a cocktail party in Paris would not imply darkness or death. At the same time, the black-and-white binary can provide some insights into perceptions of race in Western societies—for example, the historical justification of discrimination based on skin color associations.

Other deeply ingrained meanings explain the gender division or expectations about sexual behaviors (in fact, meanings of gender and sexuality are intricately intertwined). In most societies around the globe, the majority of people know what it means to be a man or a woman in the "proper way." Even though the understanding of gender roles varies from country to country and is changing over time, each person experiences pressure to be defined according to available meanings of the gender binary. Saying "I don't want to be either" will often lead to all sorts of troubles, even if this response is at times acceptable under narrowly defined circumstances (for example, hijras in India or muxes in the Mexican town of Juchitan). But in most cases, if we want to create our own unique reality where gender does not exist, we will be jerked back into the "objective world" shared by most people around us and forced to pick a side.

All that said, I am not suggesting that my readers should accept the philosophical theory of solipsism, which claims that there might be no universe external to our mind. Shared meanings do not trick us into believing an illusion. The world around us most probably exists after all, but each one of us can only partially understand it. As powerful as our minds seem to be, they can't possibly contain every single detail of what's going on in the universe. Our perspective is limited, however profound and all-encompassing it may appear to us.

In order to know the universe we all share, it is essential to acknowledge that we live in overlapping but distinct worlds. Accepting that none of us can fully access the objective reality and respecting each other's versions of it brings us one step closer to understanding what this reality actually is.

This does not mean, however, that all contradictory facts are simultaneously valid. If one person says that the sun is in the center of our solar system, but the other one claims that celestial bodies revolve around Earth, the two statements cannot be correct at the same time. The personal truths I am talking about consist of multiple interconnected *interpretations* in people's minds as well as circumstances that explain their existence. The "fact" that sun revolves around Earth seemed at some point undeniable to many serious scholars. These people were not delusional. Their perceptions cannot be viewed outside of their epoch and its limitations: available technology, scientific paradigm, religious pressures. So while not all facts can be equally justified, distinct truths should be equally taken seriously. If we discard them without investigating what's going on with empathy and curiosity, it will not be possible to piece together the big picture we all strive to grasp.

This position can be especially controversial when it comes to moral judgments. When I talk about the validity of multiple realities, I don't want to say that there is no right or wrong because everything is relative and everything goes. I am definitely not advocating for using moral relativism to say that somebody who claims they have been hurt should just shut up. This in itself would mean prioritizing one truth over others. Yet, if during a war conflict taking lives is seen as heroism by one individual and as an evil act by his adversary, the only way to understand the situation is to take both views into consideration. This is not the same as simply saying "they are both right" and moving on, which is the moral relativism that I find mostly unhelpful. However, thinking deeply about the contradictory positions in terms of relationships between various stakeholders, factors, and circumstances can bring us closer to making sense of the shared reality we all inhabit.

EGG, EGG, CHICKEN

So where do all the meanings that can influence us so much come from? How exactly does our reality emerge, whether on the personal level or as a worldview shared with others? We cannot look for an answer without trying to disentangle the knot of three factors: individual characteristics, common traits that all human beings share, and the context they live in (including social institutions with their shared goals, patterned activities, roles, and norms). Meanings attached to different aspects of our realities emerge somewhere at the intersection of the three elements. The problem is that these broadly defined components are connected in a way that makes it very difficult to determine where one begins and the other one ends. When I think about this relationship, the chicken and the egg metaphor comes to mind. Only in this case, we have two eggs and one chicken (or perhaps two chickens and one egg) to deal with.

People need to communicate—this foundational principle was established in Chapter 1. We can say that it is a common human trait embedded in our genes. However, the knowledge that is circulating in society thanks to the constant symbolic interactions is not something we are born with. Meanings are social because they are spread through everyday communication between people, shape these practices, and at the same time are influenced by them. At the same time, it would be wrong to ignore the flavor of subjectivity that shared meanings acquire as they reach each individual, who then uses them as bricks for constructing her own coherent reality.

We can say that the structure of society reflects the human nature, but also that people have evolved to their present state thanks to the social coexistence. Most probably, both claims are true. For example, the current state of society has become possible because human beings have the physiological and mental ability to use language. But our ancestors refined this capacity by living in the ancient society where language (or some prehistoric communication forms that preceded it) was already being used. What came first? We will never really know.

We may argue that our brain evolved to its current state because our forefathers and foremothers adopted tools and techniques that allowed them to introduce more meat into their diet. Our ancestors invented new approaches to hunting (including more reliable weapons) and developed better ways to cook their kill. They also learned to preserve what could not be consumed right away, so the supply of meat did not have to depend on the availability of prey and on hunters' luck. But a reverse argument could also be made. It was not the technological innovations that helped the first humans to have the high-protein diet. The diet itself allowed their brains to grow and come up with even better approaches to hunting, cooking, and food preservation.

The same what-came-first problem remains relevant when we look at the relationship between unique traits of specific individuals and more general human and social characteristics. Individual traits include our in-born temperament, mental capacities, and physical abilities. These features influence our interactions with other people as part of society but can be used, shaped, and interpreted differently according to specific environments and experiences. Think of people's skin color that determines what race they will be attributed to or genitals and associations with sexuality and gender.

We are not born as blank slates. From the very first day, we differ from each other in ways that influence our future lives. I am not talking only about skin color or genitals but also temperament and unique properties of the brain. For example, some babies are fussier than others. People around them say that they "don't have patience" or "are more emotional." Looking for words to describe such infants, grown-ups already start interpreting the trait in question and deciding what to do about it.

They may choose to fulfill the crying baby's every need or to develop his ability to wait. The context matters: whether both parents work, whether they have somebody to look after the child, etc. If the parents don't have strength or time, the needy baby will have to manage her urges, and her dissatisfaction (or resiliency) will start shaping her first associations, laying foundational bricks for her reality. As a child grows, he or she might be labeled as "more aggressive" if it is a boy and "very emotional" if it is a girl. In this case, they will be left in peace because she or he will fit assumptions about gender roles. If, on the other hand, the boy will be labeled as "very emotional" and if his parents happen to believe that men should not show their feelings, the child's experiences—and his reality—will be shaped accordingly.

An infant is born into a world that has already been organized through ideas created, changed, and maintained by other people. The child becomes fully human by internalizing these meanings. But what associations will be prominent for her and how she will use them to create her own universe is not something that could be easily predicted. Even the most powerful dominant ideologies of her culture can be experienced very differently depending on unique individual traits and the social context of her upbringing.

A girl who decides early on that she hates dresses and is persistent enough to keep fighting her gender-conforming parents will live in a reality very different from that of a girl who feels comfortable with the gender expectations of her milieu. Or that of a girl who does not want to be girly but happens to have more supportive parents. Or that of a girl who yields under pressure and wears dresses, although she still hates them. Goals, roles, and norms of a social institution we call "family" are important in determining the relationship between the child's preferences and her parents' intentions. Families are time-and-space specific, and the parenting style is an important factor in determining what dominant meanings of a certain culture are accepted or negotiated by the child.

If meanings exist in people's heads, how do we have access to them? How do these ideas make themselves known to us so that we could consider them? As we have previously established, people see themselves as meaning-*seeking* creatures, in a sense that they are trying to understand what things around them mean. But they are actually meaning-*making* creatures because objects (broadly defined) do not contain these meanings. Symbols become filled with associations as part of human interactions that we call communication. So by looking for meanings we do not discover the truth about the world but create it by sharing this world with others. In fact, the term "communication" comes from a Latin root that means "share," "have in common," or "participate in."

As a child is growing, she is learning words that help her categorize the world. She learns what "cat" is because people around her keep pointing at all sorts of cats: street cats, toy cats, pictures in books, moving images on the screen, songs ("And on that farm he had some cats/E-I-E-I-O!"). The child will learn what cats do (for instance, they purr and catch mice) and how we should act around them (cats are *not* for eating, no matter what ALF says). If the child does not have a cat at home, much of her knowledge about cats will be mediated through other people and through technology. But even when direct interactions with cats are possible, various kinds of mediation will still take place: for instance, associations will emerge through communication with close relatives who explain what to do or not to do with cats.

Earlier I suggested that we may consider language as one of the mediating tools invented by humanity. If so, we will notice that words we use also shape our understanding of the world around us. We take the existence of the word "cat" for granted, and we don't notice how it helps us distinguish them from other pets. But why are we so obsessed with differences between small fluffy mammals we call "cats" and "dogs" but call most snakes just "snakes"? Probably because we care much more about animals that share our living space than about random reptiles slithering in the wild.

So the child's meanings of cats will depend a lot on what people around her say about cats and how they act toward these moody creatures (by the way: notice how simply by using this adjective I force my associations on you). Remember that communication is often nonverbal. As we keep seeing people petting cats—but not cooking them—we naturally figure out that this is what cats are for. We could also draw some conclusions if we tried to put a cat into an oven and saw a terrified look on our parents' faces. Meanings are often communicated non-intentionally. People around us mostly just act the way they think they should, and that is how we learn that we should act this way as well.

At the same time, we cannot discard the importance of individual traits in creating our personal interpretations. People tend to divide themselves into cat- and dog-lovers. It is often hard to say how these preferences come to exist, but they probably have as much to do with our unique personalities and experiences as with any culturally shared meanings. And if someone is allergic to cats, they have additional meanings attached to these animals (although one can be allergic and still adore them).

In short, throughout our lives, we are constructing our realities based on the complicated interplay between (1) traits we were born with as unique individuals, (2) characteristics that we share with other human beings, and (3) the social context we live in (including its general as well as time-and-space-specific features). These three elements, imposed on and manifested as life experiences, determine associations we use to perceive the world. In other words, our realities emerge through human interactions, which is one of the key tenets of symbolic interactionism and social constructionism. The second fundamental principle proposed in the previous chapter—*by communicating people create the world around and within them*—is essentially a rephrased version of this statement.

People share many physical and psychological traits as they belong to the same biological species. They can have similar in born characteristics (for instance, temperament and physical abilities). Individuals can share social contexts or inhabit environments that overlap in complicated ways. I have things in common with people who live in the same time period, speak the same language, reside in the same city, who are defined by the same gender and race as me, or have the same profession. This list can go on and on, and all these intersections are important to acknowledge. They help us connect, understand, set common goals, coordinate our actions, benefit from each other's knowledge and skills. Yet, our individual realities never overlap completely, which explains all the misunderstandings and conflicts that have always been part of the human history.

I want to clarify this again: we all do occupy one *physical* reality. Its elements, from the smallest particles to mind-bogglingly enormous galaxies, move and change exactly the same way for everybody. What differs in dramatic ways is how we interpret the physical world. Meanings may seem unimportant—you cannot even touch them! But ideas in our heads define our relationship with tangible aspects of the objective universe to the point that these ideas themselves become our universe. In order to understand where these meanings come from, we have considered the interplay between the human nature, characteristics that vary from individual to individual, and multiple contexts within which we experience the physical world. In the next section, I will focus on the first one of these three elements in order to take a closer look at the third fundamental principle of communication—*it happens according to the rules of human perception and cognition.*

IT'S ONLY HUMAN

In born traits, social contexts, and experiences differ. Yet, some factors shaping attitudes and influencing behaviors are fairly consistent. I mentioned these factors before, calling them collectively "the human nature." It's time now to explain what this is supposed to mean.

Admittedly, this term is quite vague, which has allowed different thinkers to fill it up with a variety of hypotheses. Are humans essentially good or evil? Can they all be divided into males and females? Do they reproduce the image of God or instincts of the ape?[15] According to scholars who lived in the epoch of Enlightenment, what makes us human is the capabilities of our brain that have no precedents in the animal kingdom. The belief in the power of rationality influenced views and opinions of later thinkers and laymen.[16] However, I much prefer the view of Clifford Geertz, who argued that we are just animals caught in webs of meanings we ourselves have spun.[17]

It is possible to imagine that, when Neolithic people looked into the starry skies about 12,000 years ago, they felt what could be described as the shock of knowing that life is terrifying and beautiful at the same time.[18] Perhaps, it was back then that their evolving brains chose a new survival strategy. To overcome the awe and the terror of existence, our ancestors learned to make sense of it. *Make sense.* Think about this simple phrase. Peel away the layer of familiarity and feel the raw assumption behind it. It's about creating something that did not exist before, something essential for our mental balance and physical survival: order, prediction, pattern.

The Neolithic humans may have been the first ones to create meanings that explained the scary universe, including their own feelings and actions. We could also speculate that this ingenious survival strategy backfired unexpectedly. Tame ideas that were supposed to serve people by making their lives easier acquired lives of their own. Makeshift theories became unquestionable truths. Social institutions were created in order to guarantee that everyday activities will be predictable and efficient. But these institutions started imposing their rules on individuals, who felt powerless in their attempts to challenge seemingly absolute meanings.[19]

To make the matter worse, people found themselves in the constant quest for meanings, feeling the overwhelming urge to know who they were and what the next day would bring. We all have experienced it. The world needs to make sense for us, because if it doesn't, something has gone terribly wrong! This is why people say so often that things happen for a reason or why the word "meaningless" has such a negative connotation. For centuries, the development of religion, science, and art has been driven by the ultimate goal to find the meaning of life itself.

There are obviously many different characteristics—physiology, capacities of the brain, physical abilities—that we can use to define the human nature. My goal is not to cover all of them here. For the purposes of this book, I want to focus on a few traits that I believe to be key for understanding the modern media.

Following my own professional biases, I argue that the need to communicate and the ability to communicate through symbols is what makes us human. We would not have these traits if our brain did not function in certain ways. Cognitive psychologists study them by focusing on such phenomena as human perception, memory, attention, and thinking (including thinking about thinking, aka metacognition). We may venture to suggest that becoming human may have allowed our ancestors to develop these characteristics, and not the other way around. But remembering the chicken(s) and egg(s) problem from the previous section, I would not make any definitive claims.

In any case, properties of our cognitive mechanisms definitely deserve attention if we want to get closer to understanding such complex phenomena as culture and society. But this conversation is not going to be about our evolutionary accomplishments. Rather, I want to remind my readers about all the pesky glitches or shortcuts of our senses and brains, all the imperfections we have to live with. It is symptomatic that the complete list of cognitive biases has more than a hundred items (including confirmation bias, bandwagon effect, groupthink, curse of knowledge, just-world hypothesis, sunk cost fallacy, and backfire effect), which suggests that humans are not as rational as the thinkers of Enlightenment imagined them to be.[20]

One theme that becomes apparent if we explore the literature on features of human perception and cognition is that people really don't know much about how they know stuff. In other words, their own senses and brains remain a black box for most humans.[21] In his seminal book *Thinking, Fast and Slow*, Daniel Kahneman explains that we think using two cognitive systems: one is fast and intuitive and the other one is purposeful and slow. It turns out that some (actually, plenty of) cognitive processes need to stay invisible in order to be efficient, but as a result, they provide a space for hidden biases to thrive.[22] Studying the workings of morality, Jonathan Haidt came to the conclusion that the rational part of our brain is like a rider who is helping (rather than being served by) an elephant that represents our intuitions and emotional reactions. In other words, we are mostly unaware of the true origins of our own moral judgments, yet we make them all the time and even honestly believe them to be unconditional truths.[23]

Another theme is that our mental shortcuts should not be seen as universally bad, even though they can create some serious limitations when left unnoticed. While we don't have to be embarrassed for our imperfect senses and brains, it's useful to be honest to ourselves about how they really work.[24] Take, for example, implicit associations. Harvard scholars developed Implicit Association Test, which is available online for anybody willing to take it.[25] They argue that it can reveal meanings that we unconsciously attribute to different social groups. For example, creators of the test claim that most people who took it (thousands) reveal a preference for lighter skin—no matter what their own skin color is. It turns out that we don't have to be openly racist in order to feel that lighter skin is more beautiful or that it is a predictor of safety.[26] Although some have questioned whether we can really determine how biased a person is by having her take this test only once, cumulative results suggest that limiting expectations may be widespread enough to make us concerned.[27] In particular, the finding about skin colors has been used to explain discriminatory actions of police officers in the United States and has prompted many companies to provide anti-bias trainings to their employees.

Many hidden properties of the human nature are meant to make our actions faster and more efficient. Our brains and senses have evolved to help us survive (no surprises here). Our distant ancestors' brains learned to simplify information that poured in through their senses and to compare it quickly against what they already knew in order to act in a matter of seconds. Same as us, *Homo sapiens* of the ancient past relied on symbolic thinking for storing and decoding information their brains and senses produced. Similarly unaware, we use these evolutionary accomplishments every day of our lives.

Instead of seeing each object as unique (which it actually is), we perceive everything as part of a certain class or group. When a dog walks by wagging its tail, we do not focus on characteristics that make this particular animal different from anything else we have experienced. Instead, we immediately notice its "dog-ness," whether a giant St. Bernard or a tiny Chihuahua strolls by. Placing them all in the "dog" category seems like a totally obvious thing to do. But there is nothing natural about it or about the meanings it evokes in our heads. This seems harmless enough when we deal with animals. Troubles start whenever our brains apply the same shortcuts to streamline interactions with other human beings.

When you go to see a dentist, you let her perform scary and sometimes painful procedures in your mouth. You trust that dentists' goal is to help you and that your discomfort is a by-product they are trying to minimize. *Little Shop of Horrors* is probably nothing but a disturbing fantasy. Yet dentists can violate our trust in other ways, for example by persuading us to choose costly but unnecessary procedures (crowns and implants). We eat food produced in a factory whose owners supposedly know what they are doing. But if we don't regularly check ingredients of food we are buying, we may end up eating a lot of tasty but unhealthy stuff.

Discovering that people do not conform to the roles they are supposed to play can be confusing and frustrating. It can even turn our world upside down, as when the Catholic Church scandal broke loose, revealing that priests who molested children were allowed to stay in the system for years. Once we start doubting whether people we don't know perform their social roles as they should, our life becomes much more difficult. That's probably why, more often than not, we choose to believe that most social institutions around us function in our best interests.

People use skin color, profession, age, religious affiliation, gender, and many other traits to create predictions about each other. I am sure my readers are aware of many problems that these predictions cause. Each one of us has been stereotyped in one way or another, sometimes in ways that have hurt us in significant ways. Even though we see individuals we encounter as intersections of various categories, people often treat each other like boxes covered with labels, unless they get to know the contents better, and even then stereotyping can be hard to completely avoid.

The existence of the immensely complicated structure we call society would not be possible if our senses and brains did not work hard to save us time and energy while staying efficient. The human-made meanings and practices we call culture would never reach their current level of sophistication. We would not have language that allows us to share ideas and collaborate. We would not have mechanisms of tradition that enable the passing of knowledge and skills from generation to generation. But nothing that's too easy comes without a price. Maybe changing our ways would make everything easier in the end, maybe it would make the world better, but often we prefer not to try. It feels safer to keep walking the beaten path. Even if the road well-traveled does not take us to new exciting places, it is not supposed to bring us to a bear's den.

Or at least we hope so. However, some argue that by staying unaware of our brain's hidden mechanisms, we contribute not only to society's efficiency but also to its problems. Gordon Allport, who in the mid-twentieth century studied advantages and drawbacks of stereotypes, wrote: "The human mind must think with the aid of categories . . . We cannot possibly avoid this process. Orderly living depends on it." [28]At the same time, Allport warned that our tendency to categorize and simplify leads to discrimination. It turns out that we do not merely divide people into groups. We also perceive these groups through meanings that are not at all neutral. We see some people as better, smarter, or safer than others. We want everybody to conform to our expectations about them, and we feel threatened when we discover that social roles are violated.

We also use stereotypes to divide the world into "us" and "them." In the distant past, it made a lot of sense from the evolutionary point of view. It was essential (in terms of safety and mating) for the first humans to see the difference between their groups and other hominids that resided nearby. When *Homo sapiens* learned agriculture and developed the concept of wealth, it became important to see differences between conflicting groups within the same species. In the modern world, it feels good sometimes to be in a safe space with people like "us." But surrounding ourselves all the time with people who think and act the way we do means missing out on a lot of nuances. (Abraham Lincoln allegedly surrounded himself with people who disagreed with him because he understood this very well.) It means prioritizing one limited perspective on reality and rejecting a possibility that other worldviews have a reason to exist. The fact that the three men studying the elephant in the Indian tale are described as "blind" should give us a hint.

There are some specific traits essential for describing our humanity that I want to briefly touch upon here. I believe that they are important to mention due to the connection with the way we communicate through symbols. As a result, these mechanisms can help us better understand interactions happening in the modern world, especially the ones we call media.

First, there is our ability to have ideals and the tendency to be guided by them. Other animals don't bother with perfection, but we do. The ancient narratives whose echoes still resonate in our cultures were stories about the bravest heroes, the richest kings, and the most beautiful and virtuous maids. Why do ancient Greek sculptures look different from Egyptian images of pharaohs, ink drawings of ancient China, or Madonnas of Renaissance? All of them reflect not only different ways of seeing but also perceptions of ideal appearances.

By the same token, modern media representations reveal our visions of ideal men and women. These intangible ideals are a powerful presence in our lives today. The ancient Greek philosopher Plato argued that ideals actually exist and that the world of mortals is filled with their imperfect copies.[29] Nice way to rationalize the human tendency to strive for perfection! I believe that this tendency can be explained by the same abilities (and limitations) of our brains that allow us to benefit from the abstract thinking of the highest order. It is connected to cognitive traits that make seeing the world through symbols possible.

Second, there is the curious human predisposition to take for granted things we already have, and long for more. To think of it, this inclination is probably connected to the search for perfection that I have just mentioned. There is a meaning of not being/having/doing enough that we routinely attach to objects, accomplishments, and ourselves. Taking things for granted is not necessarily bad. In fact, it can be great when it encourages us to learn and grow spiritually or to create complex cultures. But more often than not, this same meaning can cause bitter dissatisfaction.

People differ (individually and culturally) in how they understand what "enough" is and in what they are willing to do in order to get it. Not everybody will pay for expensive plastic surgeries or get into debt for a better car. Alternatively, few will sacrifice their time and possibly life for what they see as social progress. The development of civilizations would not be possible without this human trait, combined with the ability to communicate our ideals to each other. Yet we can think of how the same characteristic can hurt us and those around us. We can imagine some people being lured to get things they don't need that much. Think how all of us, at times, forget that things we have without putting much effort are not necessarily available to others.[30]

Finally, a trait connected with everything described above is our urge to own—anything, really. The meanings relevant here are "mine," "not mine," and "somebody else's." You can see animals fighting for food and objects all the time, so clearly there is something primal about it. But these animals' behavior is not influenced by additional highly sophisticated ideas that people have in their heads when they decide to act recklessly in order to get an object that does not have any utilitarian application. You can see manifestations of this characteristic already in toddlers: "mine" is a word children say a lot. If you have ever observed little kids playing together (or if you have a sibling) you know what I mean. Grown-ups even had to come up with songs that have such lines as "Sharing is caring, and caring is love" to discourage their offspring from fighting over material objects. This is, of course, ironic, because grown-ups themselves do that all the time, just on a different scale.

The urge to own stuff is made stronger by the fact that we attach very specific meanings to our possessions. This tendency, "inherited" from other animals and blown to previously unheard-of proportions due to the capabilities of our brains, has caused most of the violence that has marred the human history for ages.[31] In the modern day, it has found new manifestations in the culture of consumerism. We have all known the pleasure of buying or finding something—of getting to own an object we did not have before. It is quite attractive to blame ads or the current cultural configuration called capitalism for making people want more. But is this desire really so modern? Perhaps, instead of looking for somebody or something in the contemporary world to blame, we need to ask uncomfortable questions about the human nature.

Last but not least: Imagine someone who has become fully human by growing up in society, interacting with others people, learning social practices including a language, and absorbing myriads of meanings. If this person ends up on a deserted island, we can partially understand her experiences by looking at how the human nature manifests itself on the individual level (senses and cognition). Our, say, Ronda Crusoe will try to make sense of the new environment using the existing meanings in her head. She will create new patterns and routines, rationalize her experiences, and act according to stereotypes she has about herself and the place where she is stranded. She will make an effort to adjust her environment according to some ideals in her head, even if they are merely used to describe the best shelter she can imagine. In fact, Rhonda's ability to question whether her shelter is good enough to protect her from the rain will help her stay healthy (and possibly alive). Realizing that she turned parts of the natural environment into something of her own can lift up her spirits, which can be essential for perseverance and even survival.

Yet, knowing all these features on the level of one specific individual is not enough to fully understand what it means to be human. It's only when more than one person is present that additional traits of the human nature get revealed.

Let's imagine that Ronda Crusoe is not all alone on the island. She meets another shipwreck survivor named Susan Smith. The two will start stereotyping each other, developing roles that will make their interactions predictable, fighting for possessions. In the best-case scenario, they may be able to collaborate. If not, power games will begin. Susan may trick Ronda into working harder on a shelter they are building together. Ronda may conceal from Susan a source of freshwater she found in the forest. Who decides how to make a raft? Who chooses how to use the last battery? Things can get ugly. This scenario is only hypothetical, but human struggles for power in the world of limited resources are very real.

If we want to fully understand our humanity and society, the issue of power is unavoidable. This topic, however, is too big to tackle here. We will return to it in the next chapter, which is dedicated to exploring what power is and how it manifests itself through communication.

MEDIATED MEANINGS

When you hear the word "propaganda" you probably imagine the Nazi Germany, the Soviet Union, or the world described by George Orwell in his novel *1984*. Propaganda is often understood as intentional and harmful disinformation spread widely (via technologies) in order to further one's cause. It is believed that propaganda is powerful due to its methods, such as activating strong emotions, responding to the needs of the target audience, simplifying complex ideas, and attacking opponents.[32] If your mom tells you "Don't buy this hideous sweater! You will look awful in it!" this is not propaganda, no matter how subjective your mom's opinion is, no matter how much her argument appeals to your emotions as opposed to reason, and even if the conversation is happening over the phone. Yet, some media messages designed to reach a large audience would qualify. For example, commercials (they try persuading you to buy things you do not necessarily need), but also films, TV programs, websites, journals, and podcasts created in order to promote a certain biased agenda.

If you are concerned about media, it is probably because you believe that it tells people how to think or what to do, and because you suspect that people often think or act accordingly. In this sense, propaganda seems to epitomize everything that's wrong with the media-saturated world. Most definitions of propaganda mention its intentional nature.[33] But what exactly does that mean? Does propaganda only happen when the author knows that she is spreading a lie? Even though many forms of communication are intentionally shaped to influence perceptions and behaviors, purposeful disinformation may only account for a relatively small percentage of media messages.[34] Can we then say that propaganda is an act of communication that aims to further a certain cause by persuading a large audience, no matter whether the author thinks that the information she spreads is biased or not? If the answer is yes, we may have to entertain an idea that propaganda is typical for education and social advocacy, and that its outcomes can be not only harmful but also beneficial.[35] But then again, who's to judge?

Actually, the term "propaganda" was originally used to describe a committee of cardinals of the Roman Catholic Church responsible for foreign missions. It was established by Pope Gregory XV in 1622 with the explicit goal to propagate (that is, to spread widely) the Catholic faith among peoples that had not yet seen the light. The cardinals and their subordinates were armed with printed Bibles, as at that point almost 200 years had passed since Gutenberg's invention. They also used other powerful technologies, for example, means of transportation, such as carriages and ships. And they most probably did not see their actions as controversial or harmful, even if the unfaithful had to be severely punished.

Today, for religious people, the tactics employed by the church in the past may be unacceptable, but the goal of spreading the message of God would not be at all off-point. If you believe in God, his word is not going to be misinformation for you. But for an atheist or an agnostic, the actions of imposing one's faith are propaganda indeed, whatever form they take. It all depends on our perspective. By the same token, for some people demanding more female or Black protagonists in action movies is a logical path to creating a better society. For others, it means surreptitiously promoting an agenda by activating our strong emotions while we are enjoying a movie (scripts are usually structured to make us empathize with protagonists), which means it is propaganda as well. So is a Black stormtrooper in *Star Wars* as bad as a Nazi anti-Semitic poster? For people who campaigned against the former representation, it probably is.

My goal here is not to tell you who is right and who is wrong or to define what kind of propaganda is harmful under what circumstances. Rather, I just want my readers to wonder why they prefer certain truths over others and to notice how these truths (and debates about them) can be amplified through modern technologies. We live in worlds made of meanings. When these worlds differ dramatically, they clash. And if I never try seeing beyond my own universe, other people's attempts to share their truths will only seem like harmful propaganda to me.

The process of mediating meanings is not new. Human beings have been doing that as long as they have communicated through symbols. And because symbols are created by our wondrous but imperfect brains, associations they mediate are imperfect as well. What can we do about it? The best solution is to become aware of how partial any way of representing the world to each other is. Every story is incomplete unless you take other stories into consideration, or at least acknowledge their existence and significance. Even a story filled with disproved facts—like the one told by astronomers who saw Earth as the center of the universe—must be heard. It can help us understand something important about the human history and human nature. It can even lead to better understanding of ourselves.

From the practical point of view, it means that, whenever you learn something, from any source, you should consider how this source constructs its own reality for you by describing events, people, and phenomena from a certain perspective. Even if this is a source you trust, be it your parent, your favorite news channel or author, its perspective will always be incomplete. It's much easier to notice that with sources you are already suspicious about. We label them propaganda with ease, because we feel that they are promoting a biased agenda. But remember that biases are part of the human nature, and nobody is immune to them. It also means that we need to realize how we ourselves serve as sources of information for others, promoting our worldviews that are equally partial. Your perspective, my perspective, or any other individual's perspective is never the only one possible (or correct) way of seeing the world.

Another thing we need to know about mediated meanings is that they spread best when they are easy to process.[36] This can be explained by our brain's tendency to simplify the input of the senses and by the comfort that patterns give us as a result of this quality. It's not that we don't enjoy complexity. It gives us pleasant chills. But after we dip our metaphorical toe in it, we rather prefer to go back to the comfort zone of predictability. This is why little children need routines, even though they seem to be constantly rebelling against them. This is why grown-ups enjoy rituals, even when they mock them. Archetypical characters and plotlines captivate us and connect us to each other exactly for that reason.[37]

Hollywood has been criticized for being a soulless machine that trades in shared meanings, confirming our beliefs instead of providing alternatives to archetypes. Why are female characters so often emotional, fragile, and in need of a hero? Why do male characters have to use violence for resolving conflicts? Why do protagonists often reinforce conventional beauty standards? Why are characters with darker skin seldom shown as role models? Even though all these stereotypes have recently been challenged, they still remain a concern.

Archetypical stories and clichéd characters deserve our attention not because they need to be eliminated for good, but because they can make us wonder about ideas that many people share. When we pay close attention to stories that capture attention of millions, we learn something about ourselves and about society we are a part of. It might be tempting to think that if certain meanings resonate with audiences across time, space, and ideological divides, that is because they reflect the way the world is. In a sense, they do, but this is a world created by people and it can be altered. Indeed, it's changing all the time.

Speaking about ideals: I have already mentioned the philosopher Plato of the Ancient Greece, who described a realm where they exist, a kingdom of objective truth that an ordinary person can never perceive. Instead, we are condemned to observe objects of our world. They are nothing but imperfect reflections of ideals, which are the essence of things and will forever remain outside of our reach.[38] I have to disagree with Plato because I believe that, unlike the real world, ideals exist only in our heads. They exist thanks to meanings that we share with others and allow us to say such things as "this is beautiful," "this is right," "this is real."

The media industry has received a huge share of criticism for creating an echo chamber where these meanings seem to resonate with renewed strength, allowing us to describe what it means to be a "real man," what it takes to remain attractive, or what is the right way to be a moral person. The face or the body stunning enough (in Christopher Marlowe's words) to "launch a thousand ships" may change, but the assumption that these ideals exist is not going anywhere, as well as the conviction that they can bring happiness.[39] We should see through the allure of ads that use ideals for attracting us to products and services by associating them with happiness, pleasure, and urgency. There is nothing wrong in enjoying an ideal or being inspired by it, but we should know how to use these figments of our imagination for comfort instead of frustration and wastefulness.

On the Instagram account of National Geographic Travel, I once saw a picture of a stone with enigmatic carvings. Paul Nicklen, the person who took it, provided the following caption:

> While photographing on a remote shore in northern British Columbia, I came across this rock, covered in a beautiful petroglyph. It is not known why it is there or how long it has been there. Petroglyphs were used to share a variety of messages, some including greetings, warnings, and stories. I share messages through my photography, and as I stood in this ancient rainforest, seeing this petroglyph made me feel so connected to the past—a reminder of the enduring traditions of visual communication. It's fascinating how it has evolved over time, and how the media have changed, from a carving on a rock, to a photo on your phone. But no matter how much time has passed, or how different they are, at their core is a message waiting to be interpreted.

I could not have said it better. Communication is an essential part of being human and it involves sharing messages that plant or activate meanings in people's heads. If you think that media influences you, you are right in a sense that you have become who you are through interactions with other people and through exposure to meanings mediated through symbols. But you should also remember that you have some autonomy of interpretation and that you are constantly influencing others at the same time as they are influencing you.

If you want mediated meanings not to harm you, be aware not only of other people's motives but also of your own cognitive processes. Human beings will keep inventing new ways to communicate and to affect each other. It's important to see how each new tool reflects our nature by feeding into or exploiting our biases. This does not mean that mediated communication cannot be beneficial or beautiful. By the same token, knives can cut meat for a family meal or cut human flesh during a war conflict. Media can produce harm, but it also allows us to share experiences, relax, and stay connected. We should know how to protect ourselves from meanings that may hurt us and we can do it by understanding technologies that produced them, but also by understanding ourselves.

Each person is a walking paradox. We want to stay in touch with others yet we constantly emphasize boundaries between "us" and "them." We want to learn and simultaneously to be entertained. We look for complexity, but we want it to be based on familiar patterns. If we have the freedom to challenge meanings, why do they have power over us? If you can influence other people, how come you end up being influenced by them? Our brains seem to be well-equipped to help us conquer the universe, yet they have trouble making sense of large-scale phenomena such as society itself.

In order to tackle these puzzles, in the next chapter, we are going to delve further into paradoxes of human communication. In particular, we will take a look at the aspect of the human nature and society that I have so far only hinted at: power struggles. The premise of this book is that we should not blame media, however we understand it, and instead learn more about the way we interact with each other. But not blaming is difficult if we think that somebody or something has power over us.

Even if we all participate in sharing mediated meanings, some people seem to benefit from them more than others. Shouldn't they be the ones to blame for society's flaws? We all share meanings because this is a part of the human nature, but some do it maliciously. Striving for ideals makes many people unhappy while trading in ideals brings profit to certain individuals. This does not seem right! Even if all of us are imperfect meaning-makers, it does not seem like everybody's biases get to shape society in the same way. I may be as biased as a cruel dictator, but my actions do not cause nearly as much harm.

This is all true. Yet, there is more to this story.

NOTES

1. Most of our communication in nonverbal. We often unconsciously express our thoughts and feeling through gestures, facial expressions, posture, and intonation (Pease & Pease, 2006).

2. Sloman and Fernbach (2017).

3. Here I must recognize a contradiction. According to my previous claim, limitations of our cognition and perception can usually be seen as part of evolutionary accomplishments. Keeping that in mind, I will keep calling them our imperfections, glitches, and flaws.

4. Ideas that I develop in this chapter are based on theories of symbolic interactionism (Blumer, 1969) and the social construction of reality (Berger & Luckmann, 1967). The human ability and tendency to use symbols as part of their communication is also explored within semiotics (Leeds-Hurwitz, 1993).

5. This account is based on a short documentary *The House Is Innocent* directed by Nicholas Coles.

6. It is important to note that the term "sign" can be used as a substitute for "symbol," at least in some contexts. As a subject of semiotics, signs are similar but not identical to symbols in the sense that I use for my argument. For instance, while signs (or symbols) studied by semiotics are usually described as created by humans (Nöth, 1995), I emphasize that meanings are attached to natural phenomena as well.

7. The concept of "looking-glass self" coined by Charles Horton Cooley offers additional insights into these processes (see Cooley, 1998[1902]).

8. As part of mindfulness meditation (Kabat-Zinn, 2016), you are invited to discover that emotions are actually sensations in your body and that you can change your interpretation of these sensations in order to gain control over your feelings.

9. Inzlicht and Schmader (2011).

10. Friesem and Lavi (2019), p. 89.

11. The exact quote from the book *The Interpretation of Cultures* by Clifford Geertz is: "man is an animal suspended in webs of significance he himself has spun" (Geertz, 1973, p. 5.). Geertz belonged to the field of symbolic anthropology, which is a study of cultures and societies through symbols they produce.

12. In the second half of the twentieth century, some postmodernist philosophers promoted the idea that there is no big-T Truth, as there may not even be one objective reality (Foucault, 1998[1962]). Instead of looking for this reality, we may be better off exploring why certain truths are accepted as such and how this happens. According to the sociological framework known as the social construction of reality (Berger & Luckmann, 1967), many concepts that people use to understand their world are merely products of their brains, no matter how real these ideas seem to be. We may talk about "gender," "love," and "justice" as universal notions that help us understand the world the way it is. But once we start analyzing meanings attached to these (and other) worlds by different people, it becomes evident that there is nothing universal about them. Within cognitive psychology, the focus on limitations of human rationality and the emphasis on subjectivity fits into the same trend (Haidt, 2012).

13. This quote is usually attributed to the writer Anaïs Nin.

14. The term "dominant ideology" comes from Marxism, and it has been widely used within critical cultural studies that draw on Marx's ideas about the division of society into social groups with unequally distributed power.

15. These sample questions about the human nature only scratch the surface of all the scholarly and philosophical explorations of this subject throughout the centuries.

16. Not coincidentally, the epoch of Enlightenment is also known as the Age of Reason. The term "Enlightenment" is used to describe a period of the European history that included the seventeenth and eighteenth centuries. It built on the momentum of Renaissance by further juxtaposing the power of human beings with the power of God. The key characteristic of the human being that, in the eyes of Enlightenment thinkers, made him superior to animals and closer to the divine being that created the universe, was his rationality (women were not considered too rational back then). Therefore, the human reason became the unquestionable strength, especially in comparison with emotions (that epoch was probably when the idea that men=rational are superior to women=emotional took shape).

17. Geertz (1973).

18. I borrowed the term "shock of knowing" from the book *Media, Culture, and Human Violence* by Jeff Lewis (2016). To read how Lewis explains this concept, see Chapter 1 of his book (pp. 23-50).

19. The idea about products of human creativity becoming our worst enemy is not new. Over the last century, various authors have produced fictional and scholarly narratives that explore this unsettling possibility. Most recently, in his book *Team Human* (2019) Douglas Rushkoff describes how practices and artifacts that emerged due to the human need for survival have turned against their creators. As a result, people lost awareness of their power over the complex systems their own brains had engendered.

20. For a few centuries, the idea (coming from the age of Enlightenment) that people are rational and that this is a good thing dominated the Western culture. In the beginning of the twentieth century, the pendulum swung to a different extreme as influential thinkers started suggesting that people are not rational at all (think of Freud and his idea of the unconscious mind). Today, it is almost fashionable to talk about human biases: this topic even came up during the 2016 presidential debates in the U.S. Acknowledging imperfections of our cognition is seen as the right thing to do, as a prerequisite for intellectual growth.

21. Although many of Sigmund Freud's ideas fell out of fashion, his claims about the role of the unconscious mind in human decision-making processes remain relevant.

22. Kahneman (2013).

23. Haidt (2012).

24. Assuming that we now finally know how they work, which is probably not the case.

25. The test can be found on the website of Project Implicit (https://implicit.harvard.edu/implicit).

26. Banaji and Greenwald (2013).

27. The test has become so popular that online magazines targeting non-academic audience write about it, even if only to criticize its results (Lopez, 2017).

28. Allport (1954), p. 20.

29. This idea was developed in Plato's allegory of the cave, presented in his work *Republic* (reprinted in 2018).

30. Consider the now immensely popular concept of privilege introduced by McIntosh (1990).

31. As Yuval Noah Harari notes in his book *Sapiens* (2015), every luxury tends to become a necessity for human beings over time. This makes us expect those necessities and dream of new luxuries, which leads to the justification of less than ideal behaviors that allow us to fulfil our perceived needs. One can see how this idea can be connected to the concept of privilege: same as luxuries can so easily become necessities for us, we often forget that our taken-for-granted necessities are somebody else's luxuries that they can only dream of having.

32. Hobbs (2020).

33. For a list of definitions, see the website *Mind over Media: Analyzing Contemporary Propaganda.*

34. It is important to see the difference between the term misinformation (described as unintentional deception) and disinformation (done intentionally). In other words, disinformation only happens when a person says something to somebody while thinking to herself "I am telling a lie." In contrast, misinformation describes all the instances when we tell ourselves: "I will omit those aspects of the issue and focus on these aspects to get my point across." Let's be honest, we all do that once in a while, but we don't see it as deception.

35. Hobbs (2020).

36. Starting with a simple idea, using concrete (as opposed to abstract) language, and relying on emotional stories are some of the strategies for making a compelling and memorable argument, according to the authors of *Made to Stick: Why Some Ideas Survive and Others Die* (Heath & Heath, 2007).

37. Christopher Booker argued that the underlying foundation of all narratives since ancient times is made up of seven basic plots. For example, plots that fall under the rubric of "Overcoming the Monster" include all stories about the protagonist who is trying to defeat an antagonistic force (e.g., *James Bond*). "The Quest" is about a journey filled with obstacles and temptations (e.g. *The Lord of the Rings*). And the category Booker named "Comedy" unites light stories with happy ending that is preceded by growing confusion (e.g., *Four Weddings and a Funeral*). For more information, see Booker (2019[2004]).

38. See Plato's *Republic* (reprinted in 2018).

39. Shakespeare's contemporary, playwright Christopher Marlowe used this phrase to describe the Helen of Troy, whose beauty was supposedly the cause of the Trojan war.

Chapter 3

Paradoxes of Power

The biggest criticism regarding my claim that *media is us* at this point will probably sound like this:

Yes, we all communicate and share meanings, and you can even say that we all use technology (broadly defined) to produce messages. But some people certainly have more power over how cultural meanings are formed and changed. In the capitalist society, meaning-making has become a profitable business. Look at the powerful players of the media industry, people who are calling the shots according to how much revenues meaning-peddling can bring them. Media ownership is lucrative and media conglomerates threaten diversity of ideas that circulate in the modern culture. In particular, consider those who are not only powerful but also malicious. Rupert Murdoch and Harvey Weinstein come to mind as the most villainous villains of the contemporary media world. One is the mogul who has used his information empire to influence global politics in order to increase his fortune and influence. The other one is in jail after being convicted for sex crimes that tainted everything his influential company had produced. Powerful people of this caliber and moral standards shape dominant meanings, not us—simple mortals. They use our weaknesses to build empires and silence voices that could tell stories different from their corrupted truths.

These very valid criticisms bring me to the issue of power. It's a tricky one, so I will begin tackling it from afar.

According to a curious theory known as *six degrees of separation*, all the people currently living around the globe are connected with each other through six, or fewer, acquaintances.[1] Pick any famous person and think who could link you to him or her. For example, if you are an American working for a big firm, your boss (link #1) might have interacted with a local politician (link #2). The local politician has probably met someone from

Congress (link #3). This someone from Congress might have talked to the U.S. President (link #4). And the president personally knows many famous people (link #5)! If all the links in this chain were willing to collaborate, they could pass along an envelope with a note to be delivered from you to your celebrity of choice.

Our networks of friends and acquaintances tie us all together in unpredictable ways. And yet it is next to impossible for an individual to imagine society *as a whole*. The word "society" will remain an abstraction in our heads, no matter how hard we try. Our brains are good at simplifying things, but not at processing the ever-changing complexity of the social universe we are a part of. Society is a huge and unwieldy beast, even in the present moment. And if you add the time dimension and try thinking about all the people who have ever lived as well about the future generations, it becomes truly mind-boggling. Yet even this multitude of individuals has been and will be interconnected.

In the course of our lifetime, we deal with the world of symbols, each of them bursting with meanings. We also produce symbols for others to decode—vessels to be filled with ideas. Many of these symbols are physical objects that can exist separately from us. In fact, they will exist long after we are gone. These symbols emerge every time you write a letter, take a picture, post a blog, create a drawing or a video. All of the items in this list can be called "media texts."[2]

Since we decided to define media technology broadly, media texts will include not only a photo on your Facebook wall but also hieroglyphs on walls of Egyptian pyramids. By looking at these ancient symbols, you establish a connection with people who walked the earth thousands of years ago. Even if you don't personally understand hieroglyphs, you can be sure that they have influenced the world we now live in significant ways. And in a few thousands of years, symbols on your Facebook wall might be simultaneously as enigmatic and meaningful for our descendants as the Egyptian hieroglyphs are for you today.[3]

Once we stop marveling at society's wonders, we will have to admit that it can hardly be described as a happy collective where meanings are produced, shared, and passed along for everybody's mutual benefit. People can be very loving sometimes, but they are also notoriously known for making each other suffer. Multiple scholars have pointed out that society is not just or fair, because some of its members have more opportunities than others. It is also believed that those who benefit more from the way society is (aka the status quo) are the ones who resist any positive change.

One of the most famous scholars to write about this dynamic was Karl Marx, who described capitalism as an inherently flawed economic regime built on the oppression of the working-class by the upper-class caste.[4] Throughout the twentieth century and in the beginning of the new millennium, the binary "oppressors vs. oppressed" (seen also as "villains vs. victims") has been used to talk about inequalities related to race, gender, and more.[5]

This is when the issue of power comes in. The explanation is usually simple. Society is imperfect because some (the rich, men, White people, etc.) have power over others, and they don't let the status quo change, because they like it. Communication processes are seen as part of the problem: those in power use them in order to promote meanings that make everybody accept the status quo as universally beneficial or inevitable.[6] And if somebody does not accept the situation, the power of media will be used to shut them up.

I believe that these ideas have been insightful and helped people understand some important things about themselves and others. I most certainly agree that communication reflects and reinforces power relationships that exist in society (see principle #4 described in Chapter 1). But what is power exactly? Too often, we take this term for granted without trying to complicate it—which is not surprising, considering the way our brains work. In this chapter, I suggest questioning our perspective.

We know from physics that rules of the macro world do not apply to quantum mechanics. Atoms might look like little solar systems, but subatomic particles behave nothing like planets. Einstein was actually quite disturbed by the unpredictability of the quantum world, and in his letter to Max Born, he famously stated that God "does not play dice" (meaning that same rules should apply to phenomena we see through the microscope and through the telescope).[7] I suggest that, similarly to the universe described by physics, the social world has two different but interconnected planes of existence. I argue that power struggles play out very differently whether they happen in specific relationships between people (the micro level) or in the universe of *all* relationships interconnected with each other (the macro level). Oppressors can still oppress and villains do cause harm, but when it comes to society as a whole—which we have such trouble wrapping our individual minds around—additional explanations are necessary.

POWERS THAT (MAY) BE

My husband and I once needed to go through a boring bureaucratic procedure. When we arrived to submit our documents, it turned out that one of them was missing. We were told to drive back home and bring a hard copy. It was an early winter morning and the journey did not seem particularly appealing, considering that the missing paper was not that essential (in our subjective opinion, at least). After some back-and-forth with the manager of the immigration office where the scene was taking place, we were eventually allowed to submit our documents as is.

This is a good example of how power works according to Max Weber. He defined it as "the ability of an individual or group to achieve their own goals . . . when others are trying to prevent them from realizing [these goals]."[8] In the example above, by using our power we were able to overcome the resistance of the bureaucratic machine and get what we wanted. Apparently, we could do that because we had power to use in the first place. If we had failed, it would have meant that we were powerless.

When scholars say that society is characterized by uneven distribution of power, they often mean that some people are able to achieve their goals with (relative) ease while others are more likely to hit the brick wall, no matter how hard they try. Critical theories or gender and race are built on this very premise. Those who win (men, White people, etc.) can also influence the situation in a way that ensures that they will continue winning in the future. Power is, therefore, about having opportunities and influencing outcomes.

The media is often blamed for maintaining this imbalance. Several decades ago, Gaye Tuchman came up with the concept of "symbolic annihilation" to explain how, by portraying women as less important than men, professional media producers contributed to gender inequality. (I am using the past tense, although some argue that the situation has not improved much.) Because of such media portrayals, women were doomed to have lesser opportunities for achieving their goals. They were not able to impact the direction of the world's development as much as men could. In other words, mediated communication kept women powerless.[9]

In Weber's definition that I quoted above, he talked about "an individual or a group." I believe that this is where the confusion about power begins. Social scholars and activists usually focus on the actions of individuals, but they see them as representatives of groups that have or don't have power. In these terms, a rapist's crime is a symptom of the rape culture, which can be traced back to patriarchy—the cultural configuration where women as a social group suffer from actions of generalized men. But what is this thing we call "social group" anyway?

It is worth mentioning that, as we were trying to submit our documents in the story I started this section with, it was my husband who did the arguing, and that he happens to be male and White. He could be also clearly read as heterosexual, as he was in the office with his wife (me). At the time of the bureaucratic interaction, he possessed several characteristics that, as it is believed, bring power to people who are lucky enough to belong to a powerful social group.

They can belong to it thanks to traits they were born with or to traits they choose. President Thomas Jefferson had five children with Sally Hemings, an enslaved woman of mixed race. While some of his children had to be officially freed, others passed as White and could enjoy all the privileges associated with this skin color without carrying the stigma of being a former slave. By the same token, a person who is mainly attracted to the same sex can choose to pass for heterosexual (many, indeed, have done that) in order to use opportunities that heterosexuality brings.

Other characteristics that are believed to determine power include class, religion, age, physical ability, ethnicity, and profession. So Tony, a (hypothetical) young White male heterosexual banker who comes from a rich American family, identifies as Christian and has no visible disabilities, will have substantially more doors open in front of him than Salma, an old Black Mosque-visiting lesbian janitor with a working-class background and a limp, especially if she is also an immigrant. Simple, right?

The assumption here is that the two individuals I am comparing live their lives in the United States. Watch what happens when the context changes. What if Tony and Salma end up on an island populated by dark-skinned cannibal tribes who have utmost respect for the elderly and don't care much about one's sexuality or religious beliefs? Tony might find himself in hot water, quite literally, while Salma will live many more years surrounded by care and attention. Of course, this is an imaginary situation. But then again, not all White people in the United States are bankers and not all janitors are Black. This does not mean that there is no such thing as privilege. Yet things are already getting complicated.

We like placing all people (including ourselves) into groups, with the main two—"us" vs. "them"—serving as the ultimate divider. This allows us to make convenient though possibly disturbing generalizations (e.g., men earn more money than women). In the 1980s, Kimberle Crenshaw suggested that it is essential to consider something she called "intersectionality."[10] Crenshaw used this concept to talk about dynamics of discrimination. Each person exists at the intersection of many social groups and can potentially be discriminated in several overlapping ways. For example, a Black lesbian in the United States may suffer because of her race, gender, and sexuality. Continuing this logic, we may say that intersectionality also explains how White women can oppress Black women even though both groups are oppressed by men.

However, if we take intersectionality to its logical extreme, the whole idea of dividing people into social groups becomes much less useful. Indeed, some men have it better than some women under certain circumstances. But nobody is just a woman or just a man. Each social group consists of a variety of individuals that have many things in common with representatives of groups described as opposite to them. We also often have characteristics that make us different from those with whom we supposedly share the same category. That is because social groups are constructs of our brains in the same way that meanings defining them are. This does not mean that these constructs do not have any explanatory advantages. They do, but if we blindly rely on them, they can also obscure quite a bit.

Can we always correctly point out who has power (as defined by Weber) by just looking at a person? Considering one's skin color, gender, sexuality, and other characteristics filled with socially constructed meanings can help, but only to a certain extent. Power comes and goes because characteristics attributed to us and circumstances that make these traits more or less prominent are changing all the time. In the words of Peggy McIntosh (the one who coined the influential term "privilege"),

> everybody has a combination of unearned advantage and unearned disadvantage in life. Whiteness is just one of the many variables that one can look at, starting with, for example, one's place in the birth order, or your body type, or your athletic abilities, or your relationship to written and spoken words, or your parents' places of origin, or your parents' relationship to education and to English, or what is projected onto your religious or ethnic background. We're all put ahead and behind by the circumstances of our birth. We all have a combination of both. And it changes minute by minute, depending on where we are, who we're seeing, or what we're required to do.[11]

Perhaps that's the reason why, when we feel powerful, we are simultaneously afraid to lose this feeling. We know that power will not stay with us forever, no matter how much we try. Life of the most powerful people is not stress-free: the higher you get, the harder the fall.

This complexity is the reason why I believe that Weber's definition is not enough. His wording captures correctly the fact that some individuals have more opportunities and influence than others, but it does not explain why we can say (at the risk of sounding repetitive) that powerful people don't have power over their own power. It does not describe the circumstantial nature of privilege that McIntosh pointed to in the quote above. Weber's definition is not wrong—it is incomplete. I believe that to improve it, we need to distinguish between two planes of social reality that are different from each other as much as the world of Einstein's physics was different from the quantum universe envisioned by Born.

ZOOM IN, ZOOM OUT

To describe this difference, we will need to do a thought experiment. Thought experiments are often challenging for our brains, and this one is not going to be an exception. Remember that we are trying to understand how society works on a global scale (in terms of both time and space). And that's not easy.

We will start by looking at the micro level of society, where specific interactions take place. In each of these interactions at each specific moment (the time dimension is crucial), we should be able to draw an *arrow of power* going from person A who has power toward person B who is affected by A's actions.

In order to follow my explanations, write down a few pairs of people. Parent and child. Boss and employer. Professor and student. You can get more specific: you and your daughter, your daughter and her teacher Ms. Harris, etc. Then imagine specific situations when the two people in each pair are interacting and put arrows between the names. Arrows will point from the person who has power to the one who gets to be influenced, forced, controlled. For instance, if you are telling your daughter that she cannot have a dog, the arrow will run from you to her. In contrast, when I have to wake up extra early because my toddler does not want to stay in bed (true story), the arrow will go from him to me.

Any relationship (personal or professional) consists of numerous interactions. If we examine a relationship over a period of time, as opposed to looking at one isolated moment, we can consider how often arrows of power go in each direction. When the power relationship is equal, the arrows will go each way equally often. In cases when the arrows mostly or always go in one direction, this is an indication of a power imbalance.

Talking about each individual arrow is relatively easy because each relationship in each moment is specific. We don't have to take into consideration any context (other relationships), anything that came before or will come after the moment we are focusing on. It's the kind of concreteness that our brains love.

I suggest talking about arrows in each of these isolated in time and space interactions using the term *micropower*. (You can think about it as a snapshot, so we could also call what we see *snapshot power*.) It is important to note that micropower is not necessarily used to hurt the other person (e.g., your boss telling you to prepare a file by the deadline). But it can also cause harm (e.g., your boss firing you because of your age). The main thing to understand about this kind of power is that it is what we see when we do a snapshot and zoom in on a specific interaction between two human beings.

Researchers know that any observation strategy helps us see something important but inevitably makes us miss other potentially important stuff. Relationships happen over time and in the context of many other interactions. That is why focusing on each arrow of micropower will obscure their dynamics. For instance, young kids usually have to obey when the parents say that slumber parties are prohibited till they are of a certain age. Yet, within the same family, the less digitally savvy parents might struggle to keep track of their children's activities or have any influence on their offspring's decisions in the virtual world (their interactions through social networks). This is probably frustrating for the parents, but it may also be an indicator of a balanced relationship. If kids *never* do what their parents don't want them to do, this is probably a reason for concern.

When society is described as consisting of the oppressors and the oppressed, the idea is that, whatever representatives of the two groups you take, micropower arrows will mostly run in one specific direction. In my subjective opinion, this is an oversimplification. Interactions do not take place in complete isolation from each other and each individual is not just a representative of one social group. Moreover, as I described in my introductory vignette about the six degrees of separation, everybody in society is interconnected. Specific interactions are shaped by meanings that exist in heads of people who directly participate in them as well as people who do not even know that these interactions are happening.

Interactions take place in the context of larger social institutions guided by rules that each individual person would find hard to comprehend, let alone completely subvert. For example, parents might decide to discipline their kids in a certain way because they feel that this is how families should function, even though they personally do not enjoy that. As a parent, I have been very bad at creating and following routines, but I learned how to do that because I was repeatedly told that children need routines to feel secure (whether it's true or not is a different story).

Our brains should be very comfortable analyzing each specific micropower arrow. Adding the time dimension will probably introduce some unpleasant intellectual tingling. This reaction is not unusual when we suspect that things are more complicated than we hope them to be. Introducing additional context to each interaction is bound to make the unpleasant sensation stronger. This means that our brains will be working harder to understand what is going on and to reconcile some arising contradictions. Let's see what happens if we zoom even slightly out of the level where micropower reigns supreme.

It is not difficult to imagine a manager who torments his employees but is himself tormented by his own boss; a plantation owner's wife who mistreated slaves but was abused by her husband; a king who went from signing execution orders to having his head chopped off by the guillotine. Some religious parents may feel that they need to show disapproval upon finding out that their children are not straight, because that's the meaning that they had to accept to remain a part of their religious community. Are these parents really happy about having to make this decision? Not necessarily.

As we are slowly zooming out, we will start noticing more and more arrows running between different people, determining who is affected by whom on an increasingly larger scale. This change of perspective will allow us to see relationships not only over space (so to say, from above) but also over time. This will capture what Peggy McIntosh meant when she said that the distribution of advantages and disadvantages "changes minute by minute, depending on where we are, who we're seeing, or what we're required to do." For example, a person who used to have substantial amounts of micropower when he was young may find himself losing this power as he gets older. One may feel very powerful in one community (their family circle), yet powerless if he has to deal with a different crowd (at work, in the church, army, etc.).

Cyndy Scheibe and Faith Rogow talked about this phenomenon when they wrote that

> people wield power in varying degrees. Those who lack power in one situation may have it in another (e.g., a leader may fight on behalf of oppressed people against an abusive government only to adopt oppressive policies after winning power, or an American man may enjoy the privileges of being white and wealthy but still be disadvantaged by systemic discrimination that makes him vulnerable to violence or to being fired just for being gay). In such cases, privilege is not an all-or-nothing circumstance.[12]

As we keep zooming out, our heads might start spinning as if we were rising up to the higher altitudes where the air is thin. Keeping track of our own thoughts may become increasingly difficult and the picture we see will be at the same time breathtaking and disturbing. Our minds will try keeping things simple by focusing on specific interactions, on separate arrows of micropower. Zooming out means entertaining an unsettling idea that on a larger scale a villain can be a victim, and even the other way around.

(Here I would like to briefly hit pause and discuss a concern that is possibly emerging in some of my readers' minds. The fact that a villain can be a victim does not deny the seriousness of the hurt caused by him in a specific micro situation. It does not suggest a denial of accountability. For example, even if a child molester was molested herself, her actions cannot be excused. And vice versa, even if somebody we think is "mean" becomes a victim of a crime, this should not be a reason for victim-blaming along the lines of "Serves him right!" And I definitely don't want to say that disadvantaged individuals are the ones responsible for their own troubles.)

The further away we move, the more of such paradoxical interconnections we will notice, and the least meaningful the binary villain vs. victim will become. However, we need to keep in mind that this binary does remain essential on the micro level, which we are moving further away from. This binary is not going anywhere. What we need to do is to place it in a very tricky context.

Let's now press fast-forward and zoom out the furthest we can, to the level from where the whole society could be observed at once over space and time, with all the meanings that have ever existed and will ever exist in the future. I am saying "could" because we can only try to imagine doing that, since our brains are simply unable to handle this level of detail. It is not the same as seeing the planet Earth from a space station—a precious green–and–blue ball glowing mysteriously in the emptiness of space. Rather, the kind of view I am talking about means being able to see absolutely everything, to be everywhere and to know what has been, is, and will be. It is a position of God.

How can we describe what our senses are struggling to perceive? The language is of little help as it is only a product of our imperfect brains. "It's complicated" is one generally unhelpful phrase that comes to mind. We could also say, trying to be more precise, that roots of social problems are difficult to describe, because it is not clear who has power over whom in the grand scheme of things, even if we seem to know it on the micro level.

This difficult-to-describe power that we are dealing with here is not Weber's power anymore. It does not belong to specific individuals, it cannot be used by them, but it determines what they can or cannot do. I suggest using the term *macropower* to capture this phenomenon. To explain what it is, I am going to refer to Michel Foucault. Although this French philosopher wrote quite a bit about power, he did not offer a short, easily digestible definition.[13] In fact, Foucault is known for his challenging writing style. In particular, he argued that power is like a flow and that it "is everywhere and comes from everywhere."[14] What on earth was he trying to say?

In the previous chapter, we discussed that some meanings unite many people who otherwise have very little in common (we call these meanings "dominant"). These ideas are not shared by everybody and they are subject to change, yet they are very influential. Who allows them to have this influence? People who support them. Basically, the more people believe that real men don't cry (that the Earth is round, that Jews make good violin-players and bankers, etc.), the more impactful this interpretation will be. By being a part of a *meaning community*, we accept its truth and give it power over ourselves and others. The bigger the community is, the stronger is its influence as it sucks new members in not unlike the black hole sucks in matter and light. Meaning communities of all sizes exist and expand through constant communication processes within them and outside of them, which we discussed in the previous chapter.

According to Foucault, points where power is concentrated in society at any given moment are determined by the most widely accepted truths, and by the ways of thinking and acting that these truths prescribe.[15] To translate this statement into the terms of this book, we can say that *macro*power depends on dominant meanings shared by the biggest meaning communities. At the same time, these ideas determine *micro*power—the power that specific individuals in each specific moment wield as they are interacting with each other.

If it is widely accepted that the police are guardians of peace, that they know what they are doing, and that they should be obeyed to make sure that society is not falling into chaos, police officers will have power. It is not necessary that every single person agrees with the interpretations listed above but only that *many* people do. If it is widely accepted that light skin is better than dark skin, this meaning will thrive, and darker-skinned people will keep finding themselves in all sorts of troubles (some of them of tragic dimensions). As I mentioned in the previous chapter, according to creators of the Implicit Association Test, light skin is considered to be better than dark skin by the majority of people—no matter what their skin color is.[16] Referring to this research, I definitely do not want to imply that darker-skinned people are to blame for their own misfortunes. Yet, we can see that origins and impact of cultural meanings are incredibly difficult to trace.

This is what the principle #4—*Communication reflects and reinforces power relationships that exist in society*—is about. Certain ways of being, thinking, and understanding take priority over others because of the way people interact with each other. Power may be fluid, but there are patterns to its movement, which scholars studying inequalities of gender, race, sexuality, and physical ability have explored in detail. For example, it takes a radical change of perspective to see disability as a cultural construct connected to the similarly constructed idea of normalcy.[17] Without this perspective change and a conscious effort to promote a different set of meanings, we will keep unwillingly reinforcing the idea that spaces should be primarily designed for able-bodied individuals.[18] Able-bodied people will keep enjoying their taken-for-granted privilege because of the shared social understanding of normalcy that none of them have personally created (and many of them do not entirely understand).

To put it differently, we could say that macropower is power that society has over individuals. Unfortunately, this phrasing is probably also confusing because society is made up of individuals. An arguably better phrasing would be to say that individuals are at the same time powerful (as they give power to themselves and others) and powerless (as they are constantly impacted by each other's choices and actions).[19] I believe that only grappling with this paradox will help us understand how the human society functions. This is the very big idea that I have tried to pack into the concise wording of the principle #5: *People influence each other through communication*.

To tackle this puzzle from a different angle, we could also say that macropower determines micropower but is at the same time determined by it. The structure of society, including its structural flaws, is maintained through constant interactions between numerous people connected with each other through the complex network of relationships. It is in this sense that we can argue, together with Foucault, that "power is everywhere, and it comes from everywhere," flowing through society but not staying in the same place forever.

This does not mean—to reiterate my earlier point—that abuses of power are not real or that victims of such abuses are responsible for them. Yet, considering the interplay of the micro and the macro level, I believe that "the division of the world into dualistic categories of oppressors and oppressed can lead [people] to see the world as less complex than it actually is."[20] Abuses happen on the level of micropower, which does not make them less harmful or impactful. However, to deal with these abuses, we must take the macro level into consideration.

But enough of thought experiments and abstract discussions for now. Let's take a look at some specific examples.

VICTIMS AND VILLAINS

Harvey Weinstein used to be Hollywood film producer #1. Having created Miramax with his brother back in the 1970s, he accumulated much power, money, and fame. Weinstein may have been a talented producer, but he also turned out to be a sexual predator. In 2017, he was fired from Miramax, expelled from the Academy of Motion Picture Arts and Sciences, and became Hollywood's most famous persona non grata. Weinstein's power and money did not save him, and the fame turned into notoriety.

How did Weinstein amass so much power in the first place? As Selma Hayek, one of the actresses who had suffered from his predatory behaviors, revealed in her op-ed piece for the *New York Times*, Weinstein could be nice to you or he could threaten you, depending on what he needed.[21] He knew what buttons to push and when to release them, and he masterfully navigated the media industry using his assets. Weinstein played the system well by balancing, not unlike a spider, on the web of silences that surrounded his shady actions.

While this abuser's power stemmed partially from personal characteristics, it was also given to him by other people. Those who did not question his actions. Those who knew and did not say anything either because they were not sure, or did not care, or did not take an effort to investigate further, or were afraid (not without a good reason) for their careers. It would be cruel and irresponsible to blame Weinstein's victims for his misconduct. Still, it's important to acknowledge that he was able to go unpunished for such a long time due to the actions of many different people. Most of them were definitely not trying to support these questionable activities, yet their cumulative actions became part of the problem.

Weinstein's story repeats the pattern of many other cover-ups that were widely discussed in the recent decades. Sexual abuses in the Catholic Church, cases of Sandusky and Nassar are just a few. We can be sure that plenty of other similar cases exist without the global public (or any public) knowing anything about them. The unfortunate pattern of these cover-ups can be summed up with the words: "So many people knew or suspected *something*, nobody did anything about it." I insist that this statement should not be read as blame but as the acknowledgment that seldom a villainy becomes possible solely through actions of the person who commits the villainous act. This is why the attention to the social system is essential.

In the recent years, it has become popular to talk about social problems as systemic. The theory of micro- and macropower incorporates this idea, but it also gives it a twist that may make some of us uncomfortable. This theory suggests that an individual can be singled out as an abuser of *micro*power, but he cannot be expected to determine how *macro*power works. By saying that a problem is systemic, we imply that numerous people keep it going, whether their actions are malicious, neutral, or benign.

The story of Harvey Weinstein reminds us that villains exist, and some of them get to occupy prominent positions in the media industry. But it also reminds us about the danger of generalizations. Is it ok to say that Weinstein's actions exemplify the power of White men? Some say it is. But what if we use another social group that Weinstein belongs to and argue that his actions suggest something about Jews? We could think about other influential Jewish people in Hollywood or even, more specifically, about lewd sex scandals some of them have been involved in (Woody Allen comes to mind). Suddenly, we find ourselves on a dangerous path toward anti-Semitism.[22] We might want to think twice before claiming something about *all* people working in the media industry based on the actions of a few, no matter how corrupted or malicious these few are.

"Obviously," my readers will say, "not everybody in Hollywood is like Harvey Weinstein, although abuses of power are not isolated cases, as the #metoo movement has revealed." "But," my skeptical readers will continue, "there are plenty of people who craft and spread media messages in irresponsible ways. And if these messages reach large audiences, the harm they cause cannot be underestimated. So if somebody is inconsiderate and greedy enough to sell such problematic meanings for their own benefit, they are most definitely villains responsible for society's problems." To analyze this claim, let's look at our second example.

Madonna has always been good at shocking the audience: with her looks and style, with the seemingly never-ending energy, and by exploring topics considered taboo. She has worked hard to expose the puritanism of the American culture, which is still simultaneously attracted to all issues connected with sexuality and terrified of discussing them in the open. By linking sexuality to female empowerment, Madonna has become one of the leading celebrities to promote feminist causes at the turn of the twentieth century.

As Camille Paglia put it, "Madonna has taught young women to be fully female and sexual while still exercising total control over their lives. She shows girls how to be attractive, sensual, energetic, ambitious, aggressive and funny—all at the same time."[23] But not everybody appreciates these contradictions. Critics have lamented that the singer portrays women's sexuality as their main asset. That she promotes a very specific brand of attractiveness, and that it is not clear from her message how to find the desired empowerment if one cannot or doesn't want to embrace this brand. Indeed, according to Madonna, women can do with their bodies whatever they want. However, the singer's actions may be interpreted to suggest that her female fans may want to do their best to fit certain beauty standards.

In onstage performances, red carpet appearances, official music videos, and photo shoots Madonna is often seen wearing high heels. This choice of footwear makes sense considering Madonna's philosophy of beauty. High heels are associated with female sexuality in the modern Western world, as they make legs appear thinner and longer. Yet, many health organizations point out that high heels can cause short-term pain and create long-term health problems if worn too often. They also really restrict one's movements. You can't run very fast in heels and walking long distances is practically out of the question.

How can something that hurts women and quite literally limits their movements contribute to their liberation? And if Madonna has made this something an inseparable part of her style, can we really claim that she is a "good guy" in the story of women's rights movement? Some might actually go as far as to say that this diva is a villain: she has built her entertainment empire by promoting—instead of questioning—the cultural meanings that encourage her fans to obsess over their appearance in unhealthy ways.

There is another way to see this story, another possible truth. Madonna's feminist message *is* empowering and important, but in order to promote it, the singer has to keep up with the beauty standards that she did not create. Her feet may hurt and her doctors may be filthy rich, but Madonna does not have another choice if she wants her message to stay relevant for the global audience. Perhaps, she is not a villain but a victim, a prisoner of the dominant meanings that connect female attractiveness to long legs and round buttocks?

It is true that Madonna is more visible than an average woman. In fact, she uses modern beauty standards to remain visible and loved. She benefits from these ideals as she learned how to exploit them. But she is not the one who invented them in the first place. Madonna is influenced by other female celebrities who regularly wear stilettos and towering platforms (the rebellion of Emma Thompson has been so far an exception). Madonna is not unique, as women all over the world look at each other in search of images worth imitating. And because ordinary women around the globe choose high heels, they also indirectly influence celebrities, even though famous people's impact appears to be one-directional. After all, in terms of ratio, there are many more average Janes than Madonnas, and all celebrities were at some point ordinary people themselves.

Well, Madonna does not *directly* benefit from wearing high heels, my smart reader will point out. She does not promote them, she is not selling footwear. Besides, wearing stilettos is hardly a malicious act. But how about media professionals who are not only ambitious but also immoral? Whose goal is not just to maintain their popularity but to influence people's opinions? A third example is in order.

No one epitomizes the evil and powerful machine of corporate media better than Rupert Murdoch. In the spring of 2019, the *New York Times Magazine* published a big story ominously titled "How Rupert Murdoch's Empire of Influence Remade the World."[24] It is a great piece of investigative journalism and it is definitely worth reading, but it also has some limitations, the main one of them being the uncritical description of Murdoch's power as uncontrollable.

The nutshell summary of the first (out of the three) parts of the essay reads: "Murdoch and his children have toppled governments on two continents and destabilized the most important democracy on earth" (meaning, the American one—speaking of biases). The article lays out in detail how Murdoch and his two perpetually fighting sons have impacted the political landscape of Australia, then the United Kingdom (by ushering Brexit) and the United States (by supporting republicans—in particular, Donald Trump).

Indeed, Rupert Murdoch has on many occasions used his influence to promote politicians who were willing to help his media empire grow by making it exempt from regulatory laws. He turned Fox News into a machine of ruthless republican propaganda that has spread outrageous fake news and smeared many public figures. In Great Britain, Murdoch became notoriously known for allowing (potentially, encouraging) employees of his media outlets to hack phones of celebrities, members of the royal family, and other figures of public interest. Juicy gossip acquired through such dubious channels was then used to sell millions of copies of Murdoch's tabloids, adding to his already impressive fortune.

The fact that Murdoch has power is unquestionable. He has clearly used it with ulterior motives and in morally wrong ways. But what kind of power is it? The arrows of micropower running from him to other people are numerous, meaning that his choices have affected many specific individuals, who then went on to affect others. But does he have the power to control the world, to change the course of history by shaping the global society in the ways that the *New York Times Magazine* implies (i.e., the macropower)? There are reasons to doubt that.

The wave of nationalism that has engulfed many Western countries in the recent years is hardly Murdoch's personal doing. Even the *New York Times*

Magazine admits, "The Murdoch empire did not cause this wave. But more than any single media company, it enabled it, promoted it and profited from it." Profit and political influence have been Murdoch's chief drives, to the point that he actually backed up the New Labor movement in England for a number of years (until the political landscape shifted). It is true that Murdoch has contributed to growing political polarization, but so have some liberal media outlets, as well as multiple individuals not affiliated with any media organizations simply by using social networks to communicate with each other on the daily basis. In fact, giving in to the panic about the role of media in the current polarization may distract us from looking for deeper causes of this unfortunate phenomenon.[25]

Although the *New York Times Magazine* mentions studies that found Fox News Effect ("the introduction of the network on a particular cable system [pushes] local voters to the right"), not everybody agrees about its existence. Another interpretation is that Fox News does not turn democrats into republicans but serves to reinforce the predispositions of conservative viewers (and *maybe* persuade some independents, who in the age of political polarization constitute a meager minority).[26] The *New York Times Magazine* itself argues that Fox News was created in order to cater "to those Americans whose political preferences had gone unaddressed on television news." On top of that, in order to believe that the Fox News Effect is serious enough to manipulate politically neutral or liberal voters into favoring republican politicians, we need to accept theories similar to the hypodermic needle one that I mentioned in Chapter 1. To remind you, many media scholars actually argue against the existence of uniform and predictable media effects.

Murdoch is an opportunistic businessman who has used the current social configuration of power (macropower) in order to amass personal power (micropower) for his private purposes. Political polarization and nationalism are on the rise, so he found a way to profit from them by playing the game that others have already started. It does not mean, of course, that he is innocent, as he is the one who keeps the game going. But he is not alone.

We like stories about heroes and we like being able to find someone specific to blame. But same as Martin Luther King Jr. did not single-handedly overthrow racism (which, as some say, has not been overthrown at all), powerful players of the media industry are not invincible villains who decide the world's fate sitting in Dr. Evil-esque chairs. When harm is done, their visibility allows us to point fingers at them and discuss their actions. Indeed, some of them need to be stopped and even punished. Yet, these accusations and punishments are not likely to help us get to the bottom of the problem, same as eliminating annoying and even dangerous symptoms does not cure a disease.

WHO'S IN CONTROL?

Christina Nicholson's TED Talk bears a provocative title: *Fake news: It's your fault.* As part of her message, Nicholson boldly accuses her audience of spreading misinformation online.[27] How often do we share links without comparing sources or looking for additional explanations? Actually, a lot.[28] Nicholson goes even further to claim that in the modern world all the people control media by voting down unsensational but potentially important stories simply by ignoring them. Clicks matter. They reveal what we want to do, see, and read. As a result, media outlets do not invest in investigative journalism that would dig deeper, challenge assumptions, and offer solutions.

Nicholson's position is in stark contrast with the argument presented by Eileen Meehan, the author of *Why TV is not our fault: Television programming, viewers, and who's really in control.*[29] This book is not about the same media form that Nicholson is talking about, yet I think that these two positions are worth contrasting and comparing. Meehan explains that TV ratings have nothing to do with viewers' choices and everything to do with biases of media professionals, who create content in order to sell advertising slots. She points out that Nielsen ratings, which the television industry used for decades to produce programming, were eventually determined to be misleading.[30] And even if they had been precise, preferences of viewers who were not considered desirable target audience would still have been ignored.

Nicholson's and Meehan's opinions are just tips of two icebergs—the opposites in the debate where one side claims that media has power over people and the other side argues that people have power over media. Remember the continuum of opinions about media from the first chapter? This is it again. In both cases, you can recognize the good old language of externalization. Since I personally believe that *media is people*, this dichotomy does not seem helpful to me. I see it as a version of the "us vs. them" binary that our brains are so accustomed to. Both Nicholson and Meehan do have a point—to a certain extent. They represent two different truths that need to be somehow combined in order to get us closer to understanding what is actually going on.

To help the reader see beyond the "us vs. them" dyad, the second chapter explored theories of symbolic interactionism and social construction of reality, while this chapter challenged the common assumptions about power. I chose to focus on these theories and perspectives, because they highlight one key puzzle: How can individuals shape society if society is constantly shaping individuals? In fact, this may be the ultimate question of power and control that we need to answer. When we are concerned about media or want to blame it for various social flaws, we don't think big. This is not surprising, as our brains always want to focus on something concrete.

As a result, while being preoccupied with the potential harm of specific shows, films, or Twitter accounts, we don't look at the relationship between *individual and society* as a whole. I believe that this binary is much more thought-provoking. It is also humbling. Instead of triggering blame, it encourages self-reflection. The problem is, of course, that the "individual vs. society" dichotomy makes us face the paradox of the chicken-and-egg kind that Clifford Geertz captured so well by saying that people are animals caught in the webs of meanings they themselves have spun.[31]

So who is in control after all? Is it individuals or the social system they comprise? Instead of choosing between the two sides, I suggest leaving the level of comfortable concreteness and spending some time *again* in the realm of sophisticated abstractions. On the previous pages I formulated some foundational principles of communication, of the human nature, and of social coexistence. Yet, I believe that the most basic principle that governs our existence is yet to be discussed. Focusing on it may help us answer some tricky questions that keep building up in our heads (who is to blame? who has the power over whom?), and to take another stab at the overwhelming idea of macropower.

If we peel off all the laws—written or unwritten—that govern our humanity, sociality, and culture, underneath there will be one rule of rules. It is simple: the priority is the survival of our species. This idea, obviously, is not new. It has been developed in detail by Darwin in his theory of biological evolution. Indirectly, I discussed this idea in the previous chapter by listing some intriguing human traits that can be described as evolutionary accomplishments (allowing society to survive) and at the same time as limitations (making individuals suffer). As we have discussed, in order for our brains to process information quickly and help us act effectively, most of our cognitive processes have to stay hidden from the conscious part of mind. These same hidden processes cause prejudice and our very inability to eliminate it, unless we put substantial effort into self-awareness.[32]

By the same token, the tendency to interact with the world through symbols can be understood simultaneously as an accomplishment and a limitation. You can think of it this way: turtles have shells that protect them from predators. Turtles cannot take their shells off, which can be also a limitation as shells limit turtles' movements. People have their meaning-making ability, which allows the species to survive by maintaining the systems of society and culture. Like turtles' shells, these meanings usually seem impossible to shake off. But while the meaning-making ability itself is something that we have to live with, the same is not true for specific values and beliefs, no matter how "natural" they seem to be.

Unfortunately for each one of us, our species can continue to exist even as its individual members experience confusion and discomfort. This is not my attempt to justify inequalities by saying that they serve the noble goal of saving humanity. In fact, our chances of survival may be strengthened if society learns to take proper care of all its individual members and to eliminate conflicts tearing us apart. Let's not fall back on the idea of social Darwinism with its belief in the survival of the fittest. Instead, I suggest taking a different perspective—the one that will allow us to bring this conversation back to the topic of communication. In order to do that, it can be beneficial to see the principle of survival revealing itself as the balancing act of *stability and change*, which consistently finds manifestations in social meaning-making processes.

No living organism would be able to exist if the combination of its parts and their interactions did not happen according to certain predictable patterns. Same is true for a system that is comprised of numerous living organisms. Every animal displays patterns of behavior individually and as a group. *Homo sapiens* are not very different in that sense, holding on to familiar ways of being and thinking even if those cause harm. On the other hand, for a living system to keep going, stability is not enough. It must be counterbalanced by flexibility. Species that did not have time to adapt to the changing environment have left the face of Earth forever. Stability and change are opposites, but they need to be combined in order for a living organism or a system of organisms not only to survive but also to thrive. We can imagine these opposites as the yin and yang of the Chinese philosophy—two struggling forces that are complementary and interdependent. It may seem that they are trying to annihilate each other, but without their tug-of-war life itself would not be possible.

Let's take a look at stability first. Perhaps because change can be so unpredictable and scary, the social system's impulse to maintain its core is very strong. This impulse finds numerous manifestations in individuals' lives. Most of the time, we live in a world that is (or seems to be) knowable and predictable. Although people can learn new things and sometimes drop old habits, they do the same actions with minor variations day after day. Even breaks from the routine are usually predictable. This does not mean that we live boring lives, just orderly. There is also order and stability in our brains, filled with categories that help us navigate the world.

We are all constantly contributing to society's stability by communicating to each other what things and events are supposed to mean or what different people can or cannot do. That's why norms are such a powerful presence in our lives or why it can be so difficult to leave our comfort zone and try something entirely new. Communication through technology—aka media— is not an exception. We can see patterns in all known narratives, whether they were created recently on in the past. The modern media industry is often blamed for reproducing clichés and pushing the envelope on innovative representations with the snail's speed. For better or worse, media is now a business. (Of course, spreading, modifying, or withholding information was used by some for their private benefit way before the industrial revolution.) And to stay in this business one needs to know how to confirm expectations. Why? Because people like familiarity, which promises stability.

Dominant meanings and norms often appear almost impossible to overcome, as our attempts to modify them only scratch the surface. The core does not budge, or at least it seems so. Even when longing for a change, one can still replicate good old ways of acting and thinking what he is trying to rebel against. This is true for professional media producers as well as for "ordinary" people that use technology to share and negotiate ideas.

There are two theories that I want to briefly mention here in order to provide additional insights into forces behind the social stability. One of them is called *system justification*.[33] This theory argues that people often defend and rationalize the current state of affairs due to their need for predictability and order. This need is also connected to the so-called "status quo bias," although the latter is believed to work on the level of emotions, as opposed to the rational justification.[34] Whether our heart or mind is involved, the result is the same: we prefer things to remain the way they are, even when we do not directly benefit from this. The system justification theory has one important yet counterintuitive implication. It suggests that disadvantaged individuals may support the social structure as they justify their own discomfort or feel emotionally attached to the status quo. This claim challenges the assumption that society's problems do not go away because those in power do not let that happen. I want to stress again that this is not a new variation of victim-blaming. Rather, this perspective is a way to highlight the complexity of human coexistence, which involves people contributing to the social system in various ways and for different reasons.

Guided by subconscious mechanisms of our perfectly imperfect brains, we work hard to make sense of . . . everything. We may say that whatever happens is God's will, or simply that things happen for a reason ("beyond our understanding" is often implied). Considering that, it is only logical to accept the current situation, which turns it into a self-fulfilling prophesy. Yes, things happen for a reason, but this reason is individuals' tendency to align their behaviors with what they think is inevitable (but is not). The very idea of reason or logic behind events happening around us is a product of our simplicity-loving brains. We create linear narratives out of chaos, which allows us to navigate it (=survival) but also limits us by making taken-for-granted interpretations seem the only possible truth.

Society as a whole needs to function relatively glitch-free in order for (most) individuals to live their lives and reproduce themselves, even if that means constantly struggling to find harmony in the chaotic universe. In the midst of this struggle, individuals need to be overall satisfied with their lives. Otherwise, why suffer? When we accept the way society works—which apparently can happen even when cards are stacked against us—we are less inclined to get into dangerous battles against the status quo. It is safer not to rock the boat. And when we allow the social system to exist by being part of it, we give it our unspoken consent, which is the essential idea of the second theory I want to briefly discuss here.

Consent within the theory of *hegemony* is tricky because it does not mean that we literally say "I love it" about whatever is going on. This consent—if put into words—would sound more like, "I will be a part of it, because this is the best way, because everybody seems to do it, so..." One can see parallels between this theory and system justification. If we think that there is no other (or better) way to live our lives, there won't be, simply because of our own conviction. It's those meanings in our heads at work again. They make us feel that changing the order of things we are used to is not worth trying—even if some aspects of this order annoy or even depress us.

In fact, the theory of hegemony is quite pessimistic. Which is not surprising, since its author Antonio Gramsci was imprisoned for many years under the fascist dictator Mussolini.[35] Gramsci believed that, within hegemony, the social system is impossible to modify because any attempt to do that is anticipated by the system and leads to a superficial adjustment. Combining hegemony with the theory of system justification, we can get a better idea of how this process works. Most people are overall satisfied with the status quo and/or don't want to challenge it. These "most people" are the ones who determine how the system functions. Subsequently, those who want to change things run into a brick wall.

Gramsci believed that, no matter how hard we try to undermine the flawed system—through the gradual transformation of sudden revolt—we will remain in the same place, even if it may seem different. In other words, the cultural configuration will change, but inequalities and injustices will not go anywhere.[36] The constant communication between people ensures that most of us accept the way things are and don't question them too much. Yet again, this is not an evil ploy, it's an evolutionary accomplishment helping our species to survive that is simultaneously a limitation making individuals suffer. Giving consent in this sense means supporting the current order. If there is no order, society will eventually fall apart. We may hate many things about our family, community, country, nation. Nonetheless, the impulse to participate in these groups is in most cases stronger than any discomfort we experience.

The system justification and the theory of hegemony explain how stability works, but what about change? After all, these forces are complementary. Society is not frozen in time and space. It's not made up of robots that mindlessly copy each other's behaviors. We may follow the same routine day after day but we never do it the exact same way. As the ancient wisdom goes, you cannot step into the same river twice. It won't be the same water, and it won't be the same you. This constant change on the individual level leads to the flexibility of the social system, which is as vital for its survival as its coherence. We all contribute to stability, but we also constantly question cultural meanings and tweak shared practices.

I do not think that on the global scale these changes can be described as progress or regression, as a simple journey in the "right" or "wrong" direction. Even local societies may be too complex to simply evolve or stagnate. It may be appropriate to describe their transformations as diffusion, with cultural forms traveling over space, getting appropriated, and morphing with each other. Darwin's idea of biological evolution inspired the vision of the linear cultural change, yet this may be another oversimplification created by our brains.

Cultural flexibility is with us all the time, with some modifications of practices and meanings becoming more prominent, staying around longer, or making a bigger impact than others. Artifacts produced through communication offer a wealth of evidence, as the history of material objects demonstrates. Paths of art, science and religion, variations of political regimes, fashions, and all sorts of beliefs reveal the flexibility of the human thought. When we look at social stability, it seems to be everywhere. Yet, the same thing happens when the focus is shifted to explore change. It is also everywhere, in everything we do.

It's tempting to think about social change as linear: the evolutionary development from simpler to more sophisticated forms or (if you are a pessimist) from better to worse. I believe that actual social change is multi-directional and multilayered, unpredictable and meandering. As a result, it's hard to properly describe, make sense of or evaluate.

I previously wrote that, because the modern media is a business, patterns of ideas and practices get to be constantly reproduced. But change is inevitably embedded in media representations, texts, and spaces. If we look at the history of different kinds of narratives, or of specific media forms (books, cinema, World Wide Web, etc.), we will see plenty of transformations. Some of them are associated with new forms of technology; others can be explained by changing meanings, including values and ideals. The profit motivation plays an important role in these shifts, same as in the pull for stability. Once media creators see or think that audience's interests and preferences have changed, they adjust their strategies accordingly. Not surprisingly, characters and stories that seemed perfectly acceptable several decades ago now feel laughable, insensitive, or crude.[37] Social and political activism, by playing a role in transforming worldviews, finds manifestations in media representations.

Having explored how the principle of survival shapes the human-made world through the balancing act of stability and change, we can return to the main question I am trying to answer here. Who's in control? What is this macropower that can be perceived only if we take into consideration human interactions on the global scale, over space and time? I believe that the answer to both questions is: *forces that are stronger than each of us individually but that consist of all of us—the multitude of people acting together in seemingly uncoordinated yet interconnected ways as they are balancing between the extremes of stability and change.*

Good news is that people are not powerless cogs in the social machine who only do what they are told to. However, scanning the cultural horizon in search for indications of the linear progress is likely to make us depressed. And if we insist on looking for scapegoats that impede the linear social development, we will eventually find them. Marx taught us how to do this all too well, and we are eager to use his lesson. As an optimist, I believe that each one of us can contribute to positive social change, even though it can be really difficult to do. Yet, without understanding how macropower works through the balancing act of stability and change, we will not have a map that could help us move in the direction of our choice. Worse even, we will be stuck blaming somebody or something who allegedly has power over us, instead of recognizing that this power depends in part on our own actions.

Some may say: society knows what it's doing. It is great at surviving, so we should simply let it follow its course. Don't forget about the key paradox of power: society affects us, but *it is us*, so we need to actually mind what we are doing. Society may seem like an unwieldy beast outside of our individual control. But if we let it walk blindly—if we lack awareness about our role in the social processes—the system may undermine itself and collapse. The devastating world wars of the recent history and the impact humans have on their natural habitat suggest that society as a whole may not be invincible.

All biological species have the principle of survival embedded in their genes, yet some species disappeared forever. It is my strong belief that, unless we are willing to follow their path, we must avoid blame and acknowledge that each of us has a role in the way society it, with all this intricate beauty and its flaws. Exploring in detail our own communication habits is one possible strategy for making sure that we can help ourselves and each other. This is what media literacy means for me.

This long conversation about power and control may seem like a detour in our discussion on media. Let me quickly remind you why this detour has been necessary. Our sentiments about media often take a form of blame. We are concerned that books, films, websites, commercials, and video games can shape the way we think and act in less than ideal ways. We believe that people behind media practices, spaces, and tools manipulate us for profit. Without discarding the need to look out for negative influences, I argue that relationships behind individuals, objects and processes we call media are too complicated for us to pronounce simple judgments.

The deep dive into the concept of power was meant to introduce the idea that blaming a specific somebody or something for social flaws is unproductive. If we acknowledge the strength of the pull for the cultural stability, we will be easier on ourselves and others as we are trying to make positive shifts happen. At the same time, by accepting that everybody can contribute to change, we can start considering our own responsibility for society's future.

We are all parts of the system fitting together like pieces of a puzzle, but we don't know what picture will eventually be created through our actions. Our role is a mystery to ourselves. Yet, each one of us has a role for sure and it is significant, even though we may feel stuck and confused. In the grand scheme of things we are not villains, but we are not victims either. We are what allows society to exist. And we do that by communicating meanings to each other through myriad of choices that we make on the daily basis over the course of our lives—most of them as innocent as deciding what kind of shoes to wear.

NOTES

1. This claim can be contested if we consider the existence of isolated tribes. However, in the modern world such isolated groups are becoming increasingly rare. One can certainly argue that not all the people on the planet have six or fewer connections between each other. Yet, it's undeniable that large, interconnected and overlapping social networks are essential for human co-existence (see Scott & Carrington, 2011).

2. In media studies, a *media text* is anything created to convey meanings that can be "read" or interpreted. Example of media texts include, but are not limited to: books, magazines, blog posts, films, TV programs, commercials, websites, and video games.

3. This prediction may be true, considering that everything that has ever been posted online still exists somewhere as part of the so-called "deep web" (even if it's no longer easily accessible).

4. Avineri (1968).

5. In particular, issues of power and unequal relationships between different social groups preoccupy scholars working within the field broadly defined as (critical) cultural studies (see Sardar & Van Loon, 1994).

6. Marx called this "false consciousness."

7. To clarify, in this quote Einstein was not referring to a personal God of Christianity or Judaism, but to the universal order that his own theories described.

8. As cited by de Andreis and Carioni (2019), p. 1424.

9. Tuchman (1978).

10. Crenshaw (1989).

11. McIntosh first laid out her concept of privilege in the late 1980s (see McIntosh, 1990). Although this term has become very popular over the years, McIntosh may have moved away from describing privilege as an immutable attribute of specific social groups (Rothman, 2014).

12. Scheibe and Rogow (2012), p. 232.

13. Foucault wrote extensively about power in his famous treatise *The History of Sexuality* (1998[1976]).

14. Foucault (1998[1976]), p. 63.

15. Foucault described these truths and their manifestations using to concept of "discourse" (Foucault, 1972).

16. The test and its results are discussed in detail by Banaji and Greenwald (2013).

17. Garland-Thomson (1997).

18. If you think that there is now more accessibility, try getting around in a wheelchair for a week, doing things you normally do (going to work, shopping, spending time with friends, etc.). You will be unpleasantly surprised by how difficult your life will suddenly become, as your environment will not be adjusted to your new needs.

19. This complicated relationship is explored by such theories as symbolic interactionism (Blumer, 1969) and the social construction of reality (Berger & Luckmann, 1967), which I believe to be so relevant for my argument exactly because they emphasize the said paradox.

20. Scheibe and Rogow (2012), p. 48.

21. See Hayek (2017).

22. In her talk *Did Media Literacy Backfire?* (2017) danah boyd mentioned the same danger of generalizations that we may run into when helping students develop their media literacy: "Students are also encouraged to reflect on economic and political incentives that might bias reporting. Follow the money, they are told. Now watch what happens when they are given a list of names of major power players in the East Coast news media whose names are all clearly Jewish. Welcome to an opening for anti-Semitic ideology" (para. 6).

23. Paglia (1990), para. 10.

24. Mahler and Rutenberg (2019).

25. For the analysis of the political polarization in the United States, see Mason (2018). Media has been blamed for this trend, as it is believed to create filter bubbles that keep people separated (Pariser, 2012). Although modern forms of communication can reveal and to a certain extent amplify the current polarization, I disagree that media is the main reason causing the divide. Notably, such scholars as Axel Bruns believe that these concerns are a result of a broader panic about the role of media in the modern world. In his book *Are Filter Bubbles Real?* (2019) Bruns argues that "[i]n a hyperconnected yet deeply polarised world, the most important filter remains in our heads, not in our networks" (p. 121).

26. Hopkins and Ladd (2014).

27. Nicholson (2018).

28. Vosoughi et al. (2018).

29. Meehan (2005).

30. Herrman (2011).

31. Geertz (1973), p. 5.

32. Allport (1954), Kahneman (2013).

33. Kay et al. (2009).

34. To learn more about the human tendency to support the status quo, see Eidelman and Crandall (2014).

35. Gramsci et al. (1972).

36. Gramsci called this process "co-option." In his interpretation, the dominant social system neutralizes resistance by co-opting subversive ideas. This means that the dominant system appears to accept these ideas. However, their revolutionary potential is diminished and eventually eliminated. Following this logic, one can think of how initially radical ideals of feminism were co-opted by the capitalist system. For example, some brands producing beauty products claim that women will be empowered if they use a certain mascara or lipstick. Female customers may be attracted by the idea of empowerment, forgetting that there is no indication that using this merchandise can have any effect on remaining gender inequalities.

37. For an example, see the documentary *The Problem with Apu* (2017) about the Indian-American character in the TV show *The Simpsons*.

Chapter 4

Blame Is Not the Answer

I was going to start this chapter very differently. I actually wrote half of it already— and then something unexpected happened. For the first time, I experienced fake Amazon reviews. Before this incident, I used to believe that I was good at finding quality products online. I always looked at comments and went for multiple stars. This time, I bought a set of essential oils described as "pure" as I wanted to try some aromatherapy. The product had overwhelmingly high ratings and was even marked as "Amazon's Choice." But upon receiving it, I had a strong feeling that the oils were fake: all the fragrances were overpowering in a chemical way and gave me a headache each time I tried to smell them. Even more suspicious was the fact that, once I received my purchase in the mail, the seller asked me to write a positive review in exchange for an additional set that I would get for free.

I returned the "oils" for a full refund and wrote an emotional one-star review describing my experience. A few days later, I received a note from Amazon informing me that my comment had been rejected, supposedly because I described the seller (calling their practices "manipulative") and not just the product. I did get my money back, but I wanted to help other Amazon shoppers. So I stubbornly wrote one more review focusing on the product only.

I went even further by contacting the customer service and asking them to investigate the situation with the incentivized positive reviews. I was sure that this practice should raise some red flags. An invisible Amazon representative I chatted with promised to look into the issue and notify me about the result. In a week or so after this interaction, I received a short note from the store saying that the investigation had been completed. It had determined that the set of essential oils was authentic after all, and that my second review describing them as fake was deleted. I was furious. At that point, I had done a lot of reading about essential oils and I was pretty sure that my initial assessment of the returned product was correct.[1]

What does Amazon have to do with this book's topic? Isn't it just a global online marketplace? Since its inception, this company has served as a middleman for selling a variety of products usually described as media. It started with books later expanding to music, films, magazines, video games, cameras, computers, smartphones, and other kinds of texts and technologies.[2] As Amazon was growing, it has become so much more than a store. Among other things, this behemoth of a company now offers a platform for self-publishing, produces its own shows, streams vast amounts of digital content, profits from cloud computing, and develops its version of artificial intelligence (e.g., Alexa). There is another important link to media: Amazon positions itself as a community where people can help each other choose high-quality products by writing honest reviews about them.

Amazon is a reminder that media is more complicated than we think. The definition of media I provide in this book—people communicating with each other through technology— is meant to make this complexity digestible. We should not forget that human communication comes in many forms. Online review systems are one of them. Ratings are created and accessed by people via technology. Basically, it's people exchanging subjective information and influencing each other's behavior in the process. Reviews also have a lot to do with power: whose products get sold, who gets the profit, who decides which opinions will be published, who is censored, etc. These are some of the principles of human communication listed in Chapter 1, and understanding them is essential for understanding media.

Today, reviews are an inseparable part of Amazon's identity: at its core, the company is supposed to be a "merchant meritocracy" (as one online author put it) based on transparency.[3] Having learned that it is not necessarily the case, I experienced a mix of negative emotions. I was confused when my reviews were deleted and the investigation into the product, which I was sure to be fake, led into a dead-end. I was frustrated, feeling that this unfair system would be tremendously difficult to fight. I was angry because nobody asked my opinion about the result of the investigation, which I felt had not been conducted properly. My situation was not even half as dramatic as that of many other people trampled by various "faceless" systems of our society: justice, education, military, religion, to name a few. After all, my money found its way back into my back account, so I could just move on.

But I was writing this chapter, and I had to be honest with my readers and with myself. I have encountered a flaw in mediated communication, and I wanted to find a way to do something—but do it without blame.

FAULT IN THEIR STARS

First things first: what is blaming and why do we do it? Drawing on the work of Brené Brown, I believe that blame is a natural human reaction to pain and discomfort. It's an attempt to reduce complexity and regain the feeling of control—something that we want to do so much when we feel sad, frustrated, or angry.[4] Cognitive psychologists would say that blame is a manifestation of our brains' tendency to simplify in order to help us act fast while using less energy.[5] When something bad happens, we just want to know why—the sooner the better. That's why blame does not give us time to look for deeper root causes of problems we are facing. When we blame, we are in a hurry to name a very specific guilty party, which means that answers to the recurrent "Whose fault is it?" question can be quite superficial.

Once we formulate an answer, the next logical step dictated by blame is punishing the offender or preventing them from doing whatever harm we are concerned about. Unfortunately, this means that problems we deal with are often seen in isolation from surrounding factors. We watch with utmost satisfaction how real and fictional villains get "what they deserve" in cartoonish or gruesome ways exactly for this reason. Kill the bad guy— problem solved. But is it really? My analysis of power in the previous chapter suggests that our optimism would be premature. I call it optimism to think that social issues—even the worst ones—can be traced back to specific individuals and groups of people or that big challenges of the human co-existence can be tackled separately from each other. To remind my readers, I believe that villains and victims exist on the micro level of society but not so much on the macro level of interconnectedness and interdependence.

Because human beings are meaning-makers, their brains are wired for judgment. This is another reason why we are all so good at blaming. We don't just see the world passing in front of our eyes, including our own actions and feelings.[6] Instead, we constantly form opinions about everything, which often means placing whatever we observe or experience on the "love/hate" spectrum.[7] When we blame, we get closer to the "hate" end of this continuum. It takes a substantial mental effort and a practice of self-awareness to notice how meanings that seem so natural to us are our brain's creations. In fact, it is much easier to deny that and to see our judgments as giving us access to some absolute truth about the world. I much prefer to take my cue from Martin Luther King Jr.—a known fighter against injustices—who specifically instructed his followers not to go down the path of judgment and blame that make us perceive our adversaries as enemies.[8]

I would like to add a nuance to my previous statement: blame is our reaction to *physical or emotional* discomfort and pain. Let's face it: as social beings, we experience those a lot. We might all have a certain amount of power in the grand scheme of things, but as individuals, we often feel powerless (some of us feel so more than others). Human beings constantly encounter cultural constraints and limitations they do not fully comprehend, especially since many of those are vague and fluid. As members of society, we have to negotiate the middle ground with each other, trying to make sense of contradictory needs. We want stability but are forced to deal with change. We want change but realize that it does not happen according to our plan. Each of us is like a tiny speck in the vast universe—and being a tiny speck is intimidating. We experience suffering and know that people around us suffer as well. What does this all mean? Where are we going? Faced with the incredibly complex social reality and the broader universe, we are trying to find explanations that would give us hope for easy solutions.

As we live our busy lives filled with all these struggles, we often intuitively feel that we don't have time to dig around in case of practically any troubling issue we encounter. Unless we are chased by a tiger or have somebody put a knife to our throats, we probably *could* investigate further, but easy solutions usually seem far more attractive. Since it is hard to keep all our biases in check, we let our simplicity-loving brains make a decision for us. We look around, notice whatever sticks out because it's popular, or new, or different, or just happens to be easy to reach —and make it our target. Blame is easy, but it is also unproductive because it makes us waste our energy metaphorically barking at one "guilty" tree (which may be not entirely innocent) rather than notice the whole entangled forest of causes behind it.

Media understood as objects, messages, and representations has been a target of blame due to meanings it contains. From the burning of heretical books in the Middle Ages to more recent forms of censorship, people have used their negative emotions as a justification for suppressing ideas they consider dangerous. (Whether these strategies really help to make things better is a different question).

Media can be also seen as people—usually, it's *other* people, not us. When chosen as a target of blame, they are collectively described as pushing harmful agendas, working hard to swindle and dumb down the rest of the population, doing everything to keep their power, being irresponsible, insensitive, and biased. Names of big media companies where some of these people work are pronounced with suspicion while their owners are seen as threatening figures hiding in shadows of their empires. Media industries— like Hollywood—are another blame magnet. Alternatively, we pronounce our judgments about "ordinary" media users for actions *we* supposedly would not do: spreading fake news, engaging in cyberbullying, or corrupting kids by posting commercial YouTube videos that pretend to educate.

Blame is often a way to point out a direct cause-effect relationship between actions of a certain person (or a group of people) and a negative outcome:

"Because you did A, B happened, and B is not good." But how do people hurt each other? If I stab somebody with a knife, it's pretty clear who caused the injury. Even in cases of self-defense, a wound is still a wound. But what if I say something? What if I communicate meanings in some other ways, for example, by choosing a tattoo or decorating my house with a flag? How about creating an algorithm for processing big data or buying a toy for a child? The list of subtle but essential communicative acts that we engage in every day can go on forever. It's difficult enough to explore all the gray areas it contains when we are willing to do that. Blame makes the task practically impossible.

Let's not forget that we can also direct blame toward ourselves. This does not often happen when we think about media, because we usually understand it as something existing separately from us. The idea of this chapter, as you will see soon, is not that we should blame ourselves instead of blaming others. An entirely different approach is necessary.

I am only human, so when I had my unfortunate experience with Amazon, the question "Whose fault is it?" crossed my mind almost immediately. To begin with, I had a few alternatives to choose from. First, the company as a whole: "Amazon did this to me!" (Notice that we often talk about big corporations as if they were entities having one will and one mind.) Second, I could accuse people who run this company, the most visible of them being its founder and CEO Jeff Bezos. Third, I could direct my anger toward members of the investigation team who did not address my concern. Fourth, I had an option to accuse shoppers who had written good reviews about the product I believed to be fake. Fifth, there was the seller who supplied the suspicious product with wrong description. Last but not least, I could blame myself for trusting Amazon, despite some criticism of the company that I had heard in the past. To be honest, I let my mind explore all these alternatives. But because of the approach to media and to blame that I had developed by then, I eventually chose a different route. I knew that whether I combined all these targets of blame or focused on one of them, I would miss the whole story.

The problem with blame is not that it comes from anger, sadness, or frustration. We should not suppress these emotions, because they often indicate that something must be changed. The problem is also not with speaking our mind. If we pretend that everything is ok while sitting on a volcano, we will not stop it from erupting and we will not be properly prepared for the disaster. The real issue that I have with blame is that it obscures how everything in society is interconnected. It does not allow us to see *all* people as shaping society while being shaped by it at the same time in the process of constantly communicating with each other. Blame raises important questions about power but it does not allow us to provide adequate answers.

I believe that we blame media so often because we misunderstand the basic principles of human communication and ignore how power works on the micro and macro levels. As we have established earlier, people constantly influence each other in direct and indirect ways. Society is permeated with intimately intertwined meanings that have power over us even though we have a choice to challenge them. Blaming media, we imagine objects whose negative impact can be reversed once they are destroyed, and "bad guys" who should be told to do better or leave. Yet, if we take into consideration the intricate flows of meanings that permeate the human culture, we will see that sources of pain and discomfort are not always as evident as it seems. Experiencing negative emotions is a prerequisite for change. However, when we let emotions and biases guide our actions, mistakes are almost inevitable.

BEYOND BLAME

A few days before writing these words, I threw away some old children's books that I had had as a kid growing up in the pre-perestroika Russia. I just did not feel like reading them to my sons. Closing the trash bin, I thought to myself: "Oh my, did I just do *censorship?*" Then I reasoned that this word was probably too big for what had just happened. Every parent chooses a way to teach her or his children about the world. Besides, my kids had too many books on their shelves anyways, and it seemed logical to keep only those that I truly enjoyed reading.

Some books I got rid of were just boring, but in more than a few cases, I did not find their moral lessons particularly appealing. One story was about a little frog who ran away from home to explore the world and was surprised to find his parents playing indifferent about his absence when he returned. The other one was about a girl who spent too much time dressing up in the morning because she had not arranged her clothes neatly the night before. When she came to the kindergarten late, all the children were laughing at her. In these and other narratives, I could recognize Soviet ideologies of tough love parenting and hard work.

I was not afraid of these ideas: I did not think that, if my sons encountered them one day, they would immediately adopt them. While it's fine to dislike a media text and to avoid it, we should also remind ourselves that no representation has an overwhelming effect on everybody who gets in touch with it. Many other factors are at play. And while it's ok to pick and choose what books to read to your kid, I would never advocate for banning books (that is, preventing everybody from reading them) just because I think differently. This would be real censorship, indeed. One can be angered, saddened, terrified or annoyed by somebody else's worldview and even choose to vocally condemn it. Yet it's in our own best interest to have a variety of ideas circulate in society freely.[9]

We laugh at the story of the ancient Persian king Xerxes I, who allegedly whipped the sea with a chain for having messed up with his military plans. Inanimate objects don't hurt us on purpose! Yet, we do blame a variety of objects (phones, books, etc.) we call media on a regular basis in a sense that we find a direct cause-effect connection between them and social problems. Despite what our perfectly imperfect brains tell us, this relationship is more likely to be circular than linear.[10] Because people see the world a certain way, meanings that exist in their heads are embedded in practices and outcomes of human communication. These practices and outcomes, in turn, make human-made meanings visible and available for negotiation or reproduction. When meanings are reproduced, it is likely due to the interaction between many different factors, not just because of a particular film, game, or website.

If you accept what so many media scholars agree about—media texts and representations do not have universal negative effects—then blaming these kinds of mediated communication would not make any sense to you. In fact, you may see it as a waste of time in the best-case scenario and potentially even dangerous. This does not mean that we cannot dislike some portrayals because we find them lacking in one way or another. In this case, we may encourage others to create different narratives or produce them ourselves.

Blaming media understood as people is more difficult to resist. Books and films do not make decisions, but their authors do. I could see this logic shaping my reaction in the situation with the fake reviews. I knew that I was not angry at the rating system that had misled me or at the way the online platform was structured (even though finding a way to contact Amazon representatives was annoying). No, my mind started looking for human offenders.

It is the easiest to blame somebody or something that is highly visible. Naturally, I began to read criticisms of Amazon and of its founder/CEO Jeff Bezos. There was certainly a lot of reading to do. Controversies that I found included: fake reviews, disregard to well-being of warehouse workers and delivery drivers, censorship, tax avoidance, harming the environment and small businesses, engaging in anti-competitive actions—this seemed to be just the tip of the iceberg. In addition, I saw that the company is often described as a monopoly whose growth can be explained by ruthlessness and competitiveness of Bezos—who was the richest man on the planet in 2020, a visionary leader both mysterious and suspicious.[11]

There are quite a few articles out there describing Bezos in a humorous or serious way, and almost inevitably presenting him as a potential villain in the Amazon fairy-tale growth story. Apparently, he regularly insults his employees, cares only about the bottom line, promotes aggressive lobbying, and is ready to hunt his competitors down as a predator would pursue a "sickly gazelle."[12] Oh, and how about his strange transformation around the time of mid-life crisis, his obsession with exotic foods, his weird asymmetrical eyelids?! You should admit it: blaming everything on Bezos is very attractive. After all, he is the head of the company, he determines how it's run. So if there is a problem with Amazon, it must be a problem with Bezos. In this case, we should stop racking our brains. The explanation has been found!

This thought process seems justified until we ask ourselves one simple question: What is the specific mechanism that determines how fake reviews appear on the website? Doing online research with this question in mind, I discovered something really disturbing. It looks like fake reviews have been on the rise (even though Amazon representatives say otherwise) since the company started courting Chinese sellers. This development has been correlated with the emergence of a thriving underground market where fake has become a bargain. This market does not even have to hide in the dark web to exist![13] An article published by *The Hustle* talks about "more than 150 private Facebook groups where sellers openly exchange free products (and, in many cases, commissions) for 5-star reviews, sans disclosures."[14] Some people have apparently made writing fake reviews their side job. Others may use a one-time opportunity to make some money when sellers ask them to pretty-up reviews that have already been posted on the site.

As my personal investigation continued, I noticed that my scapegoat target was becoming increasingly blurry. Of course, I could still blame the highly visible Bezos, but how about all the ordinary shoppers who saw nothing wrong with misleading fellow customers by promoting low-quality products? My mind wanted to go after Amazon, but I had to remind myself that Amazon is not *one* person. It is thousands of part-time and full-time workers with very different motivations and levels of responsibility. They are not forced to be part of this company and many of them do nothing to change it even if they don't like its practices. Knowing that many Amazon employees are overworked and underpaid, I had reasons to suspect that members of the investigation team dealing with my claim did not care much for determining the actual quality of the product in question. Perhaps they themselves were bribed by the seller, but of course there was no way to know that, because there was no transparency.

"Amazon, it's just Amazon!"—my mind kept shouting, but I was not going to give up. My solution for disrupting the blame game might seem counterintuitive. After all, I was just adding more and more potential scapegoats to the list, which was growing increasingly inconsistent. How about Bezos' inner circle—people who help him make key decisions and support the company's controversial actions, such as firing workers who went on strike about inadequate health conditions?[15] These people for sure have more power than underpaid drivers, who allegedly have to break speed limits and even to pee in bottles without leaving their vans in order to meet unrealistic delivery schedules.[16] Ok, but even the least paid workers probably had a chance to take a different job. It might not have been much better in terms of working conditions, but they would not be feeding the power-hungry behemoth. Wait, and how about all the companies that collaborate with Amazon? There are probably hundreds, even thousands of those! But then why not include in our list every individual seller who has ever sold anything through Amazon and every shopper who has ever bought stuff there?

There are already too many contradictions What to do? Let's raise our stakes. Perhaps we should just blame *capitalism*! This one is indeed a popular target among critical media scholars and progressive activists, inspired by the famous theories of Karl Marx. But then we need to add to our blame list everybody who opposes alternative economic and political systems (e.g., socialism) *and* everybody who has ever profited from capitalism and kept it going. Hm, do you know how many people that is? Most of my readers would probably have to add their names to this list as well. Even if you think that capitalism is bad, you may be quite comfortable being a part of it. And I don't blame you for that!

All right, capitalism it is. We won't be the first ones to hate it. And while we are at that, why not add classism to the mix? If you don't feel like accusing underpaid workers of becoming cogs in the Amazon machine (which is totally understandable), we can instead blame the whole system that makes these people so poor that they cannot choose what job to take. Apparently, classism is rampant in many societies even though their members deny its existence.[17] So, we will probably have to blame all those people, just in case. We don't want to miss anybody! Oh, and classism can be connected to racism, and racism is rooted in the history of the Western world big time. Classism is also reinforced by education. In the United States, poor people are mostly stuck in poor neighborhoods where their kids have to attend underfunded schools. In big cities, poor neighborhoods are often populated by people of color—so here we go, the link to racism has been established. Our list is becoming really interesting.

Onto a different target! To think of it, it is amazing how Amazon has grown from a little start-up into a multinational company. Its success is proof that competitiveness and individualism do pay off nicely, even if they hurt people in the process. Competitiveness and individualism are two important ideals of the American culture, with so many good citizens of different classes and skin colors promoting them through myriads of actions. Without diminishing the negative impact of Amazon's controversial practices, we have to agree that Bezos is exceptionally good at putting these ideals to work (at the expense of other important values perhaps, but still).

Where do competitiveness and individualism come from? If we want to investigate these ideals, many of our ancestors would have to be added to the blame list as well. You say "competitiveness"? How about the Ancient Greeks who established the famous Olympic games in order to determine who's the best? You say "individualism"? Think about Renaissance with its cult of the genius, about Reformation that gave people individual Bibles and freed minds to interpret the Holy Book independently from priests' preaching. Let's not forget about the Enlightenment that put the human mind onto a pedestal, paving the way for industrial rationality and industrial revolution. All these and many other historical developments need to be studied in order to truly understand why Amazon is the way it is or why Bezos is as feared as he is admired.

"Ok," my impatient reader will say, "So your point is that we should just blame *everybody*? Isn't that kind of useless? Find that darn scapegoat already and don't drag us into this, pleeeeese." You are so right, it is useless indeed! That was exactly the point that I was trying to make. In my humble opinion, if you want to find one perfect scapegoat in this story, there isn't one out there. Instead, there are people connected through space and time by intricate networks of meanings, people who routinely hurt each other even when they honestly try to do the best they can, people who want to do good and end up messing up, people who love and people who hate—all sorts of people, really. And the connection to media? Meanings that flow between them are often mediated through technology. Blame leads to overlooking this complexity or arguing that investigating it is a luxury we cannot afford. I believe that this kind of reasoning is a big mistake.

Once we have tried to explore the complexity that blame obscures, once we have felt overwhelmed and scared because the next step seemed to be accusing the whole world, including ourselves, we should be ready to tear our blame list into little pieces. I know, it took a long time to put it together, and you really believe that some people should stay there, but we need to let it go. If we want to think big, we should go beyond resentment. What lies on the other side?

RESPONSIBILITY AND EMPATHY

I have a confession to make: this part of the chapter was tremendously difficult to write. It was tricky enough to explain why we should move beyond blame because I had to hint at the complexity without taking the discussion too far away from the main topic. But the following step presented a way bigger challenge. I had to justify an alternative to blame which I describe here as *using empathy to acknowledge our common responsibility for what comes next*. Why did I find the task so hard? I kept reminding myself that my smart and logical readers will most certainly think of examples where blame seems to be the only option.

One such troubling case is slavery. For a person living in the United States, like I was at the time of writing this book, this word is inextricably connected with the history of enslaved Africans forced to work for colonizers of the North American continent. In fact, slavery is an ancient phenomenon that dates as far back as the flickering light of history reveals, and probably even further than that. It was slaves who built the Egyptian pyramids. Slaves also worked hard to maintain the comfort of many Ancient Greeks, including famed scholars who created the foundation of the modern science. As horrible as it sounds, the world as we know it has been significantly influenced by forced labor—both its archaic and more recent forms. I should actually say "current" because slavery still exists in many countries of the world, although it is largely considered illegal. Moreover, an estimated number of forced workers around the globe runs into millions![18]

The first thing that most likely crossed my readers' minds as I brought up this grim subject must have been: "There is no way you can blame slavery on anybody else except the actual slave owners." Not so fast! I am sure all of my readers honestly hate slavery, yet most of them have no idea that they are benefiting from its modern forms every single day. According to an article with an intentionally provocative title *Did a slave make your sneakers? The answer is: probably*, "[t]oday's slave labor doesn't look the way it did a hundred years ago. Instead, it involves poor people in developing countries trying to find work at clothing and shoe factories and finding themselves exploited."[19]

Who doesn't like a good bargain when they go shopping! But do you know that many companies are able to keep their prices affordable because they prefer not to ask difficult questions about the treatment of workers toiling away overseas? And if you think that you can solve this problem by going to more expensive stores, I have bad news for you. Some of the priciest brands, like Prada and Christian Dior, scored embarrassingly low in the past reports produced by the non-profit KnowTheChain.[20] According to this company, if consumers don't want to support the thriving global marker of forced labor, they should scrutinize not only apparel and footwear brands they use but also information and communication technology companies as well as food and beverage suppliers. This means conducting detailed research about almost every store you are entering and each product you are buying. Are you ready to do that?

The example of slavery is important because it suggests that blaming somebody specific for almost any social problem simply does not work. Once we start digging deeper and if we work hard enough, we are guaranteed to unearth some unsettling connections to actions of many well-meaning individuals, including ourselves. This example is also important for another reason: I believe that slaves are one category of people that we definitely cannot expect to share responsibility with everybody else for what comes next. It would be extremely unfair to blame them for not being able to change the flawed system they are a part of. At the same time, it is important to recognize that, like everybody else, they allow this system to exist with every breath they take.

I think that responsibility for the future is the best alternative to blame because it allows us to acknowledge our global interconnectedness while shifting focus from what went wrong to what can be improved. Responsibility for the future (known among philosophers as forward-looking responsibility) is not the same as responsibility for the past (aka backward-looking responsibility), which is synonymous with blame.[21] If you are a free person—not a slave or a prisoner, and not living under a totalitarian regime—you may exercise your power to shape meanings that eventually can determine how society functions. Even under all the terrible circumstances I have just listed, people can contribute to the state of affairs that robs them of their freedom.[22] Often these people do it because they know or feel that the price of resistance would be too high. That's why I would like to put these situations aside. But *everybody else*— and most if not all of my readers would probably fit this category—should recognize that they are not powerless in the grand scheme of things, although they can be powerless in specific situations.

Instead of finding somebody to blame for the broken system and demanding them to fix it, we should, as Gandhi famously said, be the change we want to see in the world. As most great ideas go, this is easier said than done. It would be very naive, hypocritical, and even cruel of me to suggest otherwise. If I did, I would also quite simply contradict everything I have written so far in this book. Since on the macro level of society we are all simultaneously influencing and being influenced by each other, for one individual it would be almost impossible to change the world. We create stories about superheroes and supervillains because we want to believe the opposite. For better or for worse, it's not how society works. As individuals, we are powerful and powerless at the same time—this is one of the greatest paradoxes of being human.

What I personally don't like about blame is that it doesn't provide any room for empathy.[23] Understanding the paradoxes of power requires practicing empathy toward ourselves and others. Being empathic doesn't mean not being angry, frustrated, or sad. After all, on the level of micropower, individuals do hurt and abuse each other all the time. But what good are these very important negative emotions if they don't allow us to acknowledge our global interconnectedness and common responsibility? What good is it to hate a specific slave owner in a third-world country if putting him to jail won't prevent nice people who live thousands of miles from him from buying products that allow practices of forced labor to exist?

Empathy won't force us to accept actions we don't approve of. Instead, it will help us tap into the complexity that I keep talking about throughout this volume. We can still fight against what we perceive as injustices, but our energy does not have to come from enemy images in our heads (I learned this important idea from Martin Luther King Jr. and Marshall Rosenberg).[24] We will do the world a favor if we learn to convert our negative emotions not into a hammer of righteousness but into a looking glass of curiosity. That person whose actions you despise made choices of her own under circumstances not of her own making. This is how we all live our lives, by the way. So we can hate somebody else's choices but we don't have to hate an individual who made them.[25] If you think that you are so much better than your enemy, think twice. That's exactly what happens when we blame: we think we are better than the other. The example of slavery illustrates that comparing ourselves to slave owners this way does not really guarantee that slavery will be eliminated. In fact, perhaps it is still alive and well exactly because we think we are better, and because our righteousness distracts us from investigating where our favorite sneakers came from.

Most instances of communication mediated through technology are not half as bad as slavery, although they can also produce strong negative emotions in us for a variety of reasons. One can think of a representation that portrays a social group in a diminishing way; of a journalist who produces a simplified account of an event; of an engineer who insists that an algorithm he created is completely objective; of a Twitter mob gathering their forces to "cancel" a person for saying something inappropriate; of a social media user spreading a story filled with unconfirmed facts; of a media company censoring opinions, and so on. Even in the worst of these cases, we can still learn a lot more about what's going on if we employ our empathy in order to explore other people's motivations instead of succumbing to our gut reaction of blame.

When we blame, we allow ourselves to feel superior: "I would never have acted this way!" By empathizing, we learn to recognize our shared humanity. We suspend our judgment and say: "I don't really know what this person has experienced that led him to make those choices that I dislike so much." Remember that we all are shaped by an uncountable number of communicative acts done by people around the planet. Our minds are filled with meanings that connect us to ancestors and contemporaries from all parts of the globe. That's why we can at the same time condemn somebody's decisions and trace their origins back to the web of ideas that unite us, no matter how different we are.

No individual would be able to make the world better by herself, not the least because no one on their own could tell what the perfect society would look like. History knows some unfortunate examples when groups of like-minded revolutionaries thought they had figured it all out. Because these people were so sure that they did not need to listen to other perspectives, their actions sometimes ended in tragedies that affected innumerable lives. When we are empathic toward people who hurt others in the past, we may be able to avoid running into similar problems. Empathy makes us careful and humble because it helps us see how we could make mistakes ourselves (due to social constraints and mechanisms of our brains). Empathy allows us not only to investigate others' motivations but also to acknowledge our own limitations. Nobody has all the answers.

That's where this conversation connects back to the theme of responsibility for the future. Empathy is essential for acknowledging that we are all connected through networks of communication that run across space and time. It allows us to overcome the tendency to look for somebody to blame for the status quo. We should not be too hard on ourselves for being a part of the system that is not entirely just, but it is also unproductive to hate others if they seem to have more power but don't do anything positive with it. It's micropower, remember? They can't use it to magically transform the world, and neither can you.

But the situation is not desperate. As I wrote earlier, I believe that what we all can do is use self-awareness and empathy for accepting our common responsibility for what comes next. Everybody will keep making mistakes as we are still stumbling in the dark, and some of these mistakes will be costlier than others. However, there is hope that if we truly understand how power works through communication, including its forms that we call "media," we can overcome the divisions caused by blame and create some vision of the future that will finally combine everybody's perspectives. Sounds like a utopia, I know. I guess my biggest bias is to think that it is possible.

One obvious limitation of this chapter is that I focused on just two cases—fake reviews and slavery. Because communication through technology is so multifaceted, I knew that I would not be able to analyze all its manifestations (or even the main categories) without making this discussion tedious and repetitive. It would be fair for my readers to wonder if the same logic would apply to other cases of media. I actually think that this approach should work in any situation. Whenever you start saying or thinking something along the lines of "It's their/her/his fault," I suggest that you pause and ask yourself what negative emotions you are experiencing that make you look for somebody to blame. You will need to learn to sincerely wonder about the context or any words and actions that make you unhappy. And remember that the goal of changing the perspective is not to blame yourself instead of others. Blame is not the answer.

I chose to discuss such an evil thing as slavery because I wanted to find an extreme example. Nevertheless, I suspect that my readers will easily come up with other social problems and situations where being empathic seems practically impossible. I strongly believe that, no matter how unacceptable we find somebody's actions, it is always possible to find explanations that go beyond "they are just wrong/stupid/evil" kind of response. Holding people who hurt others accountable does not have to cancel out our ability to place their actions into a bigger picture, of which we are also a part. It might seem like a stretch because it naturally makes us very uncomfortable to look for connections between choices of somebody we resent and our own decisions. I myself is still not entirely persuaded that we can *love* our enemies until the relationship between us and them transforms into something different. Yet, I do think that we can *understand* our enemies' motivations in a way that enriches our perception of the human nature, of society, and even of ourselves.[26] This deeper awareness combined with self-awareness and empathy can then allow us to communicate with each other in a way that goes beyond strife and toward new possibilities of collaboration.

In his sermon *Loving Your Enemies*, Martin Luther King Jr. tells a story of the relationship between Abraham Lincoln and Edwin Stanton, who used to be one of Lincoln's most vocal opponents.[27] To everybody's surprise, when Lincoln was elected the president of the United States, he chose Stanton as his Secretary of War. After Lincoln was assassinated a few months later, Stanton uttered the famous phrase "Now he belongs to the ages" and made one of the most beautiful statements about the president's character. Before inviting Stanton to be part of his Cabinet, Lincoln had all the right to resent him for the unkind words Stanton had said and wrote to undermine Lincoln's presidential campaign.

We can imagine Lincoln thinking to himself something along the lines of: "This guy really doesn't like me and he says hurtful things about me, but he is not a bad person. He does not think that I can be a good president. He is viciously criticizing me because he is worried for the future of the country. I can prove him wrong, but I don't have to be mean as I am doing that. In fact, I can show him that we can work together just fine to help the country we both love to thrive and prosper." I don't know if we all can necessarily collaborate with anybody we dislike (or who dislikes us), but we don't have to give up without even trying.

In closing, I want to mention that I did write the third review about the "oils" on Amazon and it stayed there. It was important for me to have my opinion represented on the platform, and I eventually got to do things my way. Moreover, I am using my micropower in the very process of writing this chapter. At the same time, I am not starting a crusade against Amazon, as I think that the idea of a global online marketplace is a good one at its core. I am still buying things on Amazon, but I also look for alternatives. I hope that one day this company will live up to its aspirations of the merchant meritocracy, by addressing this and other criticisms. This may not happen soon, considering how deeply intertwined these flaws are with the very fabric of the North American society. But there is always hope.

What's left for us to do on this intellectual journey? There have been plenty of theories and abstract discussions on the previous pages. It's time for some practical suggestions. This is what the last chapter is going to be about.

I learned from some wise friends that those who dream big can encourage other people to join in. Hopefully, my argument about the need to use empathy for collaboration across divides will make my dream appealing to at least some readers. In you are one of them, you should be appropriately curious about specific steps one can take to achieve this goal. There are plenty of things each one of us can do, really: finding out more about mechanisms of our brains, not letting our biases turn into discriminatory actions, stepping out of our comfort zone to talk—and actually listen—to people affiliated with "enemy" groups (which sometimes means just having a friendly chat with somebody who voted for a presidential candidate you did not like). Honestly, learning to have civil conversations with our own relatives during family gatherings would already be a huge step in the right direction.

I am sure you will find ways to improve methods proposed in the last chapter as you are testing them out. You will pick and choose what works for you, or you will use my general idea and look for strategies in other sources. I know that I cannot change the world by myself, cannot even claim to know how to properly do that. Hopefully, inspired by my limited view, you will find your own path. Being tiny specks in the universe should not prevent us from shaping constellations of meanings in ways that makes goodness within each one of us shine brighter.

NOTES

1. I also found other oil sets by the same company on Amazon and looked through negative reviews. There were a few comments describing the product as fake. In addition, I read more carefully the description of the oils I bought and found that in the Customer Questions & Answers the possibility of getting a free set was mentioned explicitly.

2. To find out more about Amazon's history, read Stone (2013).

3. I found the term "merchant meritocracy" in an article by Crockett (2019).

4. This idea is perfectly captured in a short animated video *Brené Brown on Blame by RSA* (2015). For more detailed discussion on blame and its connection with other key concepts developed by Brené Brown, see Brown (2010, 2015, 2019).

5. See Ariely (2010) and McRaney (2012).

6. The state called mindfulness is described as an alternative to the human tendency to form judgments about everything that is going on inside and outside of us (see Kabat-Zinn, 2016). There are some important connections between mindfulness and the ability to avoid blame, to be discussed in the next chapter.

7. We inherited this tendency from our animal ancestors. In Haidt's (2012) words: "Animal brains make such appraisals thousands of times a day with no need for conscious reasoning, all in order to optimize the brain's answer to the fundamental question of animal life: Approach or avoid?" (p. 55).

8. This idea permeates a collection of King's sermons appropriately titled *Strength to Love* (2010).

9. This claim should be considered in the context of debates about free speech, hate speech, and political correctness. Notably, the above mentioned concepts can be vague and interpreted differently under different circumstances. For example, Google's English dictionary provided by Oxford Languages defines hate speech as "abusive or threatening speech or writing that expresses prejudice against a particular group, especially on the basis of race, religion, or sexual orientation." The same dictionary defines the term "abusive" as "extremely offensive and insulting." I condemn hate speech manifested as calls for violence, as in "all X must die." However, in my opinion, not all words that some could interpret as offensive and insulting must be silenced. In order to find long-term solutions for social conflicts, we should look beyond strategies based on censorship.

10. In other words, it's a matter of complex interactions rather than a simple one-directional cause-and-effect relationship (Gauntlett, 2005; Lewis, 2016; Sternheimer, 2013).

11. For a sample of sources, see Chen (2016), Feeney (2018), Griswold (2018), Levine-Weinberg (2018), Matsakis (2018), Matsakis (2019), Porter (2018), Reimann (2020), Soper (2015), Statt (2019), and Suthivarakom (2020).

12. See Anderson (2013), Cain (2017), Edwards (2013), Jeong (2018), Stone (2013), as well as Streitfeld and Haughney (2013).

13. Dark web itself is not illegal, although some specific sites that exist there are. Notably, dark web requires special browsers to access it.

14. Crockett (2019).

15. Greene (2020), Wood (2020).

16. Peterson (2018), Roberts (2017).

17. Isenberg (2017).

18. According to a British non-profit organization Anti-Slavery, "40 million people are estimated to be trapped in modern slavery worldwide" (see the page "What Is Modern Slavery?").

19. Segran (2018).

20. The report citing this finding was created in 2018 (Segran, 2018). In 2020, KnowTheChain was working on a new assessment, and the old report was no longer available on their website.

21. For some insights about these terms, see van de Poel (2011).

22. Václav Havel in his essay *The Power of the Powerless* (1985) described how ordinary citizens oppressed by a totalitarian regime can either contribute to the status quo or attempt to undermine it.

23. It was thanks to Brené Brown's work that I started thinking about blame and empathy as the opposites.

24. King (2010), Rosenberg (2015).

25. Separating people from problems their actions appear to be causing is an age-old wisdom. Fisher, Ury, and Patton used it in their bestseller *Getting to Yes: Negotiating Agreement Without Giving In* (2011[1981]), which suggests that this empathy-based strategy can actually help those who use it to achieve their goals.

26. The difference between cognitive and emotional empathy implies that we don't have to agree with somebody in order to understand their actions. For a scholarly discussion explaining this binary, see Perry and Shamay-Tsoory (2013).

27. This sermon is included in the collection *Strength to Love* by King (2010).

Chapter 5

ACE It

If you think of it, virtually all human knowledge about the world is mediated. It means that whatever we know (or think we know) about ourselves and others is filtered through several layers: our senses, our brains, ideas of a culture we inhabit, the language we use, and all sorts of technologies that exist outside of our bodies. This is why understanding media—in the broadest sense of the word as well as in the more specific "modern" one—is so important. It allows us to see with more clarity where our truths and facts come from, which can ideally help us become more careful with ideas we share, more open-minded, and more empathic.

In a way, it is actually great that most of our knowledge comes through mediated communication. It means that, so to say, *you don't have to be there to be aware*. We don't need to invent the wheel: our ancestors did that for us. That, and so many other great things we can learn about by listening to our parents, going to school, reading, surfing the Internet, or just talking to each other. By the same token, we do not need to get into a car accident in order to know why driving carefully is important. Being aware in this sense saves us time. It often saves our lives! Another aspect of awareness is defined as a "concern about and well-informed interest in a particular situation or development."[1] It is certainly an advantage that we do not have to personally deal with a problem (a disease, poverty, sexual violence, etc.) in order to know that it exists and to be willing to do something to minimize its negative influence.

On the other hand, exactly because our knowledge is mediated, this by itself creates a host of problems. What we know depends on what part of the metaphorical elephant we have touched. Truths each of us communicates to others can only be partial. Awareness is colored by our biases, shaped by individual traits, and reflects the cultural milieu we exist in. By ignoring these nuances, we risk taking the route of blame or choosing actions that will lead us in the wrong direction. On top of that, instead of propelling us to do something, knowledge can be confusing, scary, depressing, and paralyzing. Awareness can make us want to curl up in a corner or fill us with crushing certainty that may cause more damage than good.[2]

In the previous chapters, my goal was not only to enhance my readers' understanding of the modern media. It was to show the importance of reflecting on what it means to be part of society, what it means to be human. I wanted you to consider the limitations of our senses and brains in order to see how our imperfections determine the way the social system is. I realize that thinking about our role in the world from this perspective can be upsetting and annoying. We all want to do good but if the chance of messing up is so high, why even try? Clearly, *self*-awareness can also lead to sadness and passivity, or turn into endless navel-gazing. It is important to remember that knowledge—whether about ourselves or the broader universe—may lead to sorrow, if not handled properly.[3]

To deal with these challenges, we should take into consideration the new understanding of communication and power that this book was meant to provide. Being aware of an unfortunate social issue is evidently a prerequisite to resolving it. However, it is not helpful if one sees such a problem but ignores its connections to a variety of immediately and distantly related circumstances, as well as to numerous people's actions, whether malicious or benign. An individual by herself or as part of a group may have some understanding of the situation but forget how dangerous it is to rely only on one truth and leave out other possible interpretations (however contradictory they may seem). A strategy based on such a partial view can yield visible results in the short run. Yet, if we don't consider the complexity of factors, over time a proposed solution will create new problems. Humanity has been playing this game of whack-a-mole for quite a while now. In order to put an end to it, it is essential to engage in major-scale collaboration efforts between people with different ideologies, experiences, and approaches. At its core, such collaboration must have a free exchange of ideas—sharing and negotiation of meanings unhindered by censorship or prejudice.

I am convinced that a path toward such collaboration lies through empathy. Honing and using this skill would allow us to see our opponents as potential allies, and not just "bad" or "stupid" people, which is a sentiment that leads us toward increasing polarization. As I wrote before, I am not sure we can truly love our enemies (as long as *enemies* they remain) yet we can aspire to learn from them, or at least about them. In this case, our goal should be not to triumph over our adversaries but to enrich our understanding of the problem we are trying to solve by infusing it with viewpoints different from our own.

Ideally, this understanding can help us find common values and indicate ways to work across all sorts of divides.

Last but not least, empathy can also minimize the negative effects of awareness that I mentioned earlier, such as passivity and fear. Once we put ourselves in other people's shoes, even when the size seems completely off, we may find this experience unexpectedly soothing. It is good to know that our opponents are people with whom we can potentially find a common language. On the other hand, self-empathy can encourage us to fight thoughts that paralyze action. We can acknowledge our biases while not beating ourselves up for having them. Likewise, you do not have to give up on causes you believe in order to admit how hard it is not to contribute to the status quo.

This is the rationale for a model I am going to describe in this chapter. It is called ACE: from Awareness to Collaboration through Empathy. The following sections will address the three elements one by one, proposing some specific strategies I learned from others (mediated communication!) and tested through personal experience.

AWARENESS: MEDIA LITERACY

Although my book is very different from the body of literature within the field of media literacy, I hope that the connection is clear.[4] In the broadest sense of the word, literacy means "competence or knowledge in a specified area."[5] By writing this book, I was hoping to provide my readers with insights about media, to enhance their knowledge about it. Perhaps unexpectedly, this process involved challenging assumptions about communication, technology, society, and even ourselves. I am greatly indebted to the media literacy community, of which I consider myself a part, for inspiring me to apply critical thinking to various forms of mediated communication that I encounter in my daily life. Since I see media as people communicating with each other through technology, in this book, I tried to expand my readers' understanding of what it means to be human.

My favorite tool for increasing all kinds of awareness that I am happy to recommend to my readers is a set of questions that one can use to analyze various examples of mediated communication.[6] You can find different versions of this instrument proposed by various scholars and practitioners.[7] I personally love the simplicity of a set formulated by my friend and mentor, media literacy guru Renee Hobbs. For this chapter, I took her Media Literacy Smartphone exercise and slightly changed the wording to account for a variety of media forms that I want you to be able to examine.[8] Here are the questions:

1) Who created this and why?
2) What techniques are used to attract and hold attention?
3) What values, assumptions, lifestyles, and points of view are embedded?
4) How may different people interpret or use this differently?
5) What is hidden or omitted?

In this section, we will practice using these questions together. For starters, let's do the following exercise. It will help you come up with instances of media you can analyze. Take a piece of paper and write out different *types* of media. We will begin by listing some important categories without examples. Here are the categories that I suggest considering:

• Media text (e.g., book, film, magazine, or TV program)
• Media representation (e.g., character, place, or event)
• Media tool (e.g., physical object or digital application)
• Media space (e.g., social network or game)
• Media channel (any media outlet)
• Media message (e.g., specific phrase, image)
• Media practice (what we can do with or via the items listed above)

Now, think of two to three examples for every category and write them down row by row, like I did below. I encourage you to come up with some instances of media you love and some you are suspicious about. In other words, don't only list thing you are eager to criticize. Also, you should feel free to go beyond the modern media.

• Media text: *Frozen*, the Bible, "Scream" by Munch
• Media representation: China in *Mulan* (1998), Botticelli's Venus, accounts of the Hurricane Katrina
• Media tool: iPhone, sculpting chisel, language
• Media space: Twitter, World of Warcraft, dark web
• Media channel: Fox News, HuffPost
• Media message: "You snooze, you lose," swastika
• Media practice: texting, reading, vlogging

As you are creating your list, you might notice that the division of mediated communication into various types feels artificial. Because media is such a complicated phenomenon, the categories I provide are meant to help us deconstruct it. We should not forget, however, that categorization always reduces complexity. After all, media tools are used to create media texts and messages; texts and spaces contain representations; channels spread multiple texts, messages, and representations, while people access them via media tools, etc. Canadian scholar Marshall McLuhan, who significantly influenced the development of the media literacy field, famously wrote: "The medium is the message."[9] This much-quoted phrase implies that media tools and channels can be difficult to disconnect from messages produced through them or from corresponding production practices.

Now you can look at the media literacy questions again and practice answering them about any item on your list you find particularly intriguing. Don't be intimidated by this task. I don't expect you to provide comprehensive answers right away, or even at all. The best approach will be to give some preliminary responses right now and to see if you can learn more as time goes. To do that, you will need to keep the questions in mind. If you are really serious about the task, consider sticking them on the wall or carrying with you in the form of the Media Literacy Smartphone.[10] The goal of this activity is not to find the ultimate truth but to develop lifelong skills of expanding our awareness through inquiry.

I know that you are probably eager to dissect that news channel you think is run by greedy crooks or a portrayal that seems to be dangerously off. You can indeed do that to warm up. But I am afraid to tell you that the most learning will happen when you analyze media items you trust and love. This does not mean you have to force yourself to hate these examples. The activity I am describing is about finding new ways to look at familiar things.

1. Who created this and why?

The first part of this question seems simple enough. For example, if you take a book from a shelf, you will easily find the name of the person who wrote it. In this sense, some media items have a single author while others have plenty. However, it's also not unusual to encounter a practice, text, or message whose creators' names we cannot locate.

Certain idiomatic phrases are used by many, but their origins are virtually impossible to trace. Folk proverbs and sayings existed through word-of-mouth before they were written down, thus going from one medium (spoken language) to another (books). Maybe there is one person behind each idiom—the one who actually uttered it first—but it took thousands of communication acts to connect you to her or him. Same is true for some basic media practices, such as reading and writing. Who invented them? I think it is safe to say that we will never know. These literacy skills evolved through generations of people who honed them while developing corresponding tools.

Well-known visual messages can be equally mysterious. Did you know that swastika is actually an ancient image that represented the sun and divinity in Indian religions? In Western world, this symbol was associated with prosperity and good luck till the 1930s, when the Nazi Party in Germany adopted it for its campaign. The ancient authors of swastika will remain unknown because its roots go too deep into the humanity's past, but the journey this visual message made to get to our modern collective imagination is intriguing to say the least.

One may argue that the closer we get to the current time, the easier it will be to say who the exact creator is. For instance, naming people who invented iPhone must be a piece of cake! So who are they? "Apple or Steve Jobs," you may say. Alas, these responses will be incomplete if not inaccurate. First, there were (still are) many teams within this company who have developed different aspects of the ingenious smartphone. Second, assembling this highly complicated piece of technology would have been impossible without numerous contributors, many of them having nothing to do with Apple. Such aspects of iPhone as the touch screen, rechargeable lithium battery, and even its dependence on the World Wide Web have required collaboration between more people than you can imagine.[11] This example suggests that it may be useful to make a distinction between immediate authors and numerous contributors who influenced the development of a certain media instance.

French literacy critic and postmodern philosopher Roland Barthes wrote an essay titled *The Death of the Author*, where he argued that any literary work is made of intricately layered cultural meanings.[12] Its interpretation, therefore, cannot begin and end with deciphering the author's intent, pointing out her biases, experiences, and values. I am the author of this book in a sense that I wrote it all by myself. Yet, I have drawn on ideas of multiple people who thought about the things discussed here recently or well before I was born. My book would not be possible without them, and the bibliography at the end of this volume serves as a reminder of my intellectual debt and a form of gratitude. Taken to extremes, this line of thinking suggests that even the most comprehensive list cannot contain names of all people whose actions shaped the text in question.

I would venture to claim that Barthes' argument can be applied to media outside of the realm of literature. The case of iPhone described above provides a good illustration. We look for authors as some kind of all-powerful creatures who weave the fabric of cultural meanings all by themselves. If some meanings cause harm, we blame their obvious creators. It's useful to consider that immediate authors may hold *micro*power as they benefit from texts or representations they are producing—but not *macro*power over the processes that determine what ideas and practices will be accepted or become popular.

Once the tentative list of authors has been compiled, you can explore their motivations. I should probably say, you can *try* to explore them. Motivations are even more difficult to know than names of all the contributors, for one apparent reason. You cannot get into somebody else's head, so you have to infer the intent based on observable results of their actions. According to Barthes, you cannot ever know the author's intent—only form your interpretations of it. Nonetheless, this does not mean that any investigation is futile.

A novice may be surprised to discover how many instances of mediated communication are shaped by the imperative to make profit. This is true for the modern era as well as for more traditional media versions. For instance, famous painters and sculptors of the past produced their masterpieces not just because they were visited by a muse. In the most prosaic way, they needed to earn their living—which they often did by pleasing rich patrons and customers. How different is this from the imperative to please real or imaginary audiences that modern media professionals follow in order to keep their jobs? Generally, making potential audiences and users happy is a crucial motivation for many immediate authors. Profit does not even have to be part of the equation as creators' decisions are shaped by their perception of what other people may think or say.

A savvy media scholar would know about the media economy for sure. On the other hand, she may run the risk of forgetting that revenues are not the only thing that determines why and how people "do" media, even on the large commercial scale. There is no contradiction in wanting to promote a certain idea because the author thinks it is right or creating something she considers beautiful *and* looking for ways to make money in the process. Even the most innovative representations need to be attractive for the public in order to reach it. The argument can be made, of course, that in the media industry the profit motivation comes first; media professionals justify their creations (it terms of their moral and aesthetic value) as an afterthought. This may well be true in more than a few cases. Another thing to keep in mind is that, in case of large commercial projects, the resulting text, space, or practice can reflect contradictory motivations of all the different people behind it.

The question about contributors and their goals remains relevant when you yourself become a media producer—which happens whenever you share something on social networks, send an email, create an app, or leave a graffiti on the wall. You certainly know who *you* are. But are you aware of at least some of your hidden co-authors? Do you really know how your culture, community, and language speak through you? Understanding your motivation may require some vulnerability. Remember that there is nothing inherently bad in wanting to make your product marketable. It is important to keep in mind that the quest for something as simple as attention—not just fame and big money—will shape the way you are communicating your ideas, no matter how neutral they appear to be. Exploring one's own implicit intent may take some soul-searching and courage.

2. What techniques are used to attract and hold attention?

Since mediated communication happens all the time, why do only some of its outcomes get noticed, used, or remembered? Several thousand new tweets appear every second. Most of them will be known only by a few, despite their availability. New media tools are being regularly invented, but only some become truly popular. Identities of immediate authors play an important role: when a famous actor writes something on social media, there is a bigger chance for his words to start conversations around the globe than if I write a blog post. But fame is something one has to achieve and maintain. There are plenty of people out there competing for audience's attention. Whatever the motivation is, one needs to think creatively how she will grab the interest of potential customers, consumers, and users.

Attention is a precious resource, and the battle for it can get vicious.[13] Not everybody is equally good at this game. One interpretation of such disparity is that those who win have more power to begin with because of their social characteristics (gender, race, etc.). These traits are, indeed, important to consider. However, the amount of interacting participants it takes to make a media message, text, tool, or space popular suggests that the *macro*power plays an essential role in the attention economy as well. In other words, it's not just about actions or characteristics of one individual creator or even a team of them. When an idea starts making waves, you can be sure that its immediate authors did something that resonated with other people's expectations and met their needs.[14]

When you look at a media space, channel, or practice, it's helpful to ask what specific techniques have been used to ensure its popularity. It's equally beneficial to wonder why these techniques work to begin with. A media space may become a new sensation if it manages to help users stay connected, get entertained, or express themselves particularly well. There is something about apparent efficiency of functions that can attract the global community, because these features take into consideration our need for simplicity. A media text will be enjoyed by multiple audience members if it manages to apply familiar tropes in seemingly innovative ways. A message built to arouse people's emotions and provide simple explanations may go a longer way than one that appeals to reason by subverting our preconceived notions. A new practice would not become part of many people's lives if it does not give users what they already want, consciously or subliminally.

It takes some effort to recognize tricks of the attention economy in each specific instance. Here are some things you may want to do to develop this skill.

Open your favorite website and look at its visual elements. Even the smallest details matter. What colors are used and how? Where is the text located?

How is the navigation structured? There is a reason developers spend hours organizing layouts and test-driving them to perfection. Of course, websites are not pictures to look at, so functions must be also appealing. It can be enlightening to see how Facebook has been changing options that users have for registering their reactions. The "like" button is now iconic. But have you ever thought why providing an opportunity to share the way one feels about certain content makes an online networking space more attractive?

On to a different medium. When you are watching a movie or an episode of a TV show, notice elements of the plot structure that make you want to know what happens next. Find characters' traits that render them relatable or fun to observe. Dialogue makes a tremendous difference, as does music in the background. You may not even notice how crucial these audio aspects are, but if you turn the sound off, your experience will be quite different. There is a whole science of camera movements that only a person versed in filmmaking understands, and it works like magic. Meaning, you may not even notice how you are getting enchanted, pulled into an alternative universe of the story you are experiencing. And when you are under a spell, asking critical questions is extremely hard.

Many people form so-called parasocial relationships with characters or actors who play them. These fictional and real celebrities may evoke in us a feeling of deep connection, even love. Under these circumstances, criticizing them will seem like a crime, same as when somebody says unpleasant things about your beloved spouse or offspring. All this can happen because our attention has been so thoroughly captivated. That's exactly why we need to be able to break the spell and challenge ourselves to notice aspects of media stories that we find particularly irresistible.

In fact, storytelling itself is an age-old attention-grabbing technique. There is something about the human brain that makes narratives fascinating for us.[15] One form of media where this human tendency is currently exploited is news. We often don't care much about general information describing an event (statistics and such). But give us a personal story that's going through the stages similar to those of an ancient Greek tragedy and we will be hooked.[16] So the third activity that will help you practice thinking about the attention economy can be this. From now on—as you are watching news or reading journalistic investigations—notice how often they follow a specific protagonist whose experiences can be described using the classic narrative arc: exposition > rising action > climax > resolution. (As a side note, effective documentaries use the same strategy.)

If you want to be a successful communicator, you need to have a simple message that will appeal to your target audience's feelings and needs by telling them emotional yet credible stories filled with unexpected facts.[17] At the same time, it's good to remember all these techniques also make for effective propaganda.[18] For this reason, it is essential to remain self-aware as we are communicating ideas, no matter how deeply we believe in them. I am not going to tell you to avoid creating memorable messages or texts that will enchant your readers and viewers. By all means, do so. But remember that, even though uniform media effects do not exist, you are going to influence other people in multiple ways. This is another reason why attention should be considered precious, even priceless.

3. What values, assumptions, lifestyles, and points of view are embedded?

Here is one simple fact that my readers will find difficult to argue with: all people have values. In other words, everybody has something that's important to them. These beliefs and ideals determine our everyday actions and shape big life-changing decisions. This seems intuitive enough. What you might have not considered is that values infuse whatever you communicate to the world, whether on purpose or not. It's of course up to others how to interpret your words and actions. One person does not necessarily understand what is important for another one; even if she does, that may not change her own worldview or course of action.

And yet, noticing values embedded in a variety of media forms is not a waste of time. Such activity can be both intellectually stimulating and instructive. Although we don't automatically start sharing others' beliefs once we find ourselves in their orbit, we can certainly be influenced by these ideas, especially if we are (or want to be) a part of a certain community. If you grow up surrounded by people who firmly believe that one must be independent and self-reliant, you will most likely feel that way too. On the contrary, if your culture prioritizes group needs over individual freedoms, this state of affairs will seem quite natural to you. The invisible and taken-for-granted nature of values should not come as a surprise after we have so thoroughly discussed features of human-made meanings.

All processes and outcomes of mediated communication, if properly examined, *may* reveal something about what's important for their creators—or what their creators think is important for target audiences and users. In fact, when media authors can properly guess values of whoever they are trying to reach, the attention economy game is half won. You won't be using a media tool or spending time in a media space if they don't provide what you appreciate or crave. At the same time, following Roland Bathes, I believe that any definitive conclusions must be avoided. There is always a big "probably" hanging in the air. But we can still carefully speculate.

The history of media tools and practices reveals the tendency to invent new ways for people to learn from each other, connect, and spread information.

These are our fundamental human needs, so it's not surprising that they find various manifestations in consciously or subconsciously communicated values. For instance, if we consider the written word as one of the basic media technologies (the one that Socrates was allegedly so concerned about), we can discern in it the value of creating reliable records, unifying knowledge, and passing information from one generation to another.[19] The modern world is much more fast-paced than the society built by ancient Greeks was. Speed and efficiency are now held in high esteem in many cultures around the globe. It is logical that these environments have produced new variations of writing down and sharing our ideas, such as email. So before you curse an inventor of the electronic messaging system that keeps you writing responses and clicking "Send" all day long, consider how this form of media reflects the current cultural configuration.

Different forms of mediated communication can also potentially reveal something about points of view, assumptions, and lifestyles of people who created them, or people who enjoy them. In 2013, the non-profit organization Pro Infirmis produced a campaign "Because who is perfect? Get closer." The video representing the campaign on YouTube shows five people with various visible disabilities.[20] First, we see mannequins created in their likeness and then observe these mannequins being placed in windows of a fashionable store for passersby to discover. This campaign was praised as an innovative way to fight against the stigma of disability. Without diminishing the merits of the approach used by Pro Infirmis, we can take a critical perspective to try inferring how effective this approach may have been.[21]

For example, we can notice that the video sometimes clearly takes the point of view of a person without disabilities, especially in the scene where the participants' measurements are taken. As this is done (by somebody without any visible disability), differences are framed as deficiencies as in "38cm missing" and "only three toes." One assumption hidden in this emotional video is that displaying bodies with visible disabilities in a place where "normal" bodies are usually seen is a significant step in the fight against ableism. Another assumption is that onlookers who discovered these unusual mannequins while passing by the storefront changed their perspective on disability (and were not simply confused or shocked). These and other assumptions are not explicitly stated, which makes it difficult to question them, especially for viewers caught in their emotions watching this moving visual sequence.

As for the lifestyle, a careful observer would notice that the new mannequins are dressed in clothes suitable for a cocktail party: a black dress on one and a white shirt plus black bow tie on the other one. These outfits evoke associations with the middle and upper class. Moreover, by choosing mannequins and store windows for conveying its message, creators of the campaign present consumerism as the natural (or desirable) way of life, which of course it does not have to be.

When authors' values, assumptions, lifestyles, and points of view are similar to ours, it's easy to overlook them as something totally commonsensical. Here is a very different example. One day I was going to defrost some prepackaged shrimp. Instructions on the plastic bag said: "Hold under running water for 10 minutes." This simple message contained a hidden assumption that having water run for 10 minutes is a perfectly normal and harmless thing to do. In the past, I used to share this assumption as I come from Russia, where being wasteful with water is not seen as a problem (or at least it was not when I lived there). Yet, since then I have learned from my husband that water is a precious resource. In Israel, where he comes from, this value is an essential part of the culture. I ended up just soaking the shrimp for 10 minutes in a bowl of water, and they were just fine.

Things we take for granted are by definition hard to notice, whether they are embedded in words and actions of others, or in our own communication practices. Don't try questioning all your own hidden values and assumptions here and now, because it would be impossible to do. This will either lead to frustration or to the feeling of complacency (if you think you have succeeded). The habit of such self-reflection should be developed over time. For starters, it's good to acknowledge that most of your opinions and beliefs remain invisible to you, posing as "just the way things are." Hidden points of view may be easier to notice in moments of crisis, life-changing decisions, and conflicts. But beware that in all these cases heightened emotions can prevent us from doing self-reflection. Alternatively, you can focus on small disagreements, like the one I initially had with my husband when he told me that I am spending too much water. These disagreements, when properly approached, can help you face other people's realities and wonder about origins of your own truths.

4. How may different people interpret or use this differently?

As a person coming from Russia, I am very sensitive to stereotypes of my compatriots in media texts. Not because these portrayals feel offensive. They just take away from my experience. For instance, I find Russian villains in U.S. films simply ridiculous. When they are supposed to be menacing, I often want to laugh. At the same time, it's hard for me to evaluate authenticity of representations when it comes to Indian, French, Mexican, Egyptian—well, any other culture except the one I grew up in. It's the same with stories about people whose experiences are similar to mine—for example, scholars, educators, immigrants, and parents. While sometimes I can be tickled by the pleasant feeling of recognition, it's often irritating to see familiar matters being distorted or ignored. It helps to keep these reactions in mind when somebody else says they hate a media representation that seems perfectly harmless—or even informative and useful—to me.

Of course, individual experiences differ even when it comes to people united by a certain trait. One person cannot speak for everybody in a group she feels a part of.[22] Yet, it's not a trifle when somebody says that their community is mis- or underrepresented. There may not be an easy solution to this problem because perfect media portrayals do not exist. On the other hand, even the most stereotypical depiction out there probably corresponds to somebody's reality. Still, I would not take it lightly when people lament that their stories are not properly told or that they don't feel seen. If you constantly encountered limiting stereotypes of your community in media texts, you would not be happy either.

Wondering about other people's perceptions of various media forms can help us better understand lives distinct from ours. It is refreshing to realize that your way of seeing the world and being in it is not universal. At the same time, we should approach this task carefully. There is always a temptation to declare: "Well, of course, other people have their own points of view, but mine is the correct one. They just don't know enough!" It is important to be curious about possible interpretations without becoming judgmental or feeling superior.

The situation is similar with media uses. A friend of mine keeps TV programs running as a background noise. For me, either a program is on and I am watching it—or off and I am doing something else. But then I have to acknowledge that many programs are now made to be consumed the way my friend does it! By the same token, some modern media tools—for example, computers—have so many uses that it should not be surprising to see another person focusing on functions you don't even consider important. Same as with interpretations, avoiding judgments about others' media use can expand your horizons. For examples, teachers can see smartphones merely as a distraction in the classroom or they can think of activities that would allow students to practice research skills on their own devices.[23]

We should become careful observers and pay attention to what other people do with or say about mediated communication. Because we all reside in our own neat bubbles, it can be hard to see things from a perspective unusual for you without any help. Sometimes the simple act of listening can do the trick. Remember all those passionate debates that you participated in or witnessed about merits of books, films, or TV programs? Perhaps, instead of just insisting on your opinion, you can ask questions that would give you more insight into your opponent's argument: "Could you tell me more about the way you understand/apply this?"

I believe that one realm where such curiosity is sorely needed is politics. In the current climate of vicious polarization, we can often think of only one reason why our opponents have a different understanding of a media outlet we love: "They are just stupid." I don't expect my readers to overcome this gut reaction with ease. Yet you should at least *try* to consider what life experiences could lead somebody on the other side of the political spectrum to develop media uses and interpretations different from yours. (Suggestion: don't focus on mental retardation and fatally flawed morality.)[24] While we are still talking about awareness here, the fourth question on our list should make it easier to see a connection with the next stage of the ACE model— empathy. Just remember that you don't have to lose yourself in other people's perceptions and practices. The goal is not to devalue your point of view but to enrich it.

When you communicate mediated ideas yourself, it's useful to consider other people's interpretations and uses for two main reasons. First, you will be able to avoid the so-called curse of knowledge. It's a good practice not to assume that other people know things you do.[25] This will help you improve your arguments, tell compelling stories, and provide necessary (but not redundant) explanations. Second, you will be able to avoid or at least minimize harm by reminding yourself to choose your words carefully, honor other voices, and respect worldviews different from yours. At the same time, it's good to remember that you cannot please everybody. It's impossible to predict all uses and interpretations, no matter how hard you try. You will not make your message perfect, but you can do your best.

5. What is hidden or omitted?

Though we all inhabit our unique worlds, (mediated) communication offers a window one can use to peek into another person's universe. Windows are great for seeing what's going on inside, but don't think that they can reveal everything. You will be looking from a certain standpoint, and your view will be limited by the frame. As a result, some objects and aspects will remain hidden, so you will need to do some guesswork. Invisibility does not equal the lack of significance. Some things are too sacred or obvious, others may be taboo for reasons that are important to scrutinize.

No media message, text, or representation can comprehensively cover their subject. This is not a flaw. No matter how hard you try, you will not be able to include each possible detail and angle. A story about everything would be a story about nothing. Take for instance, a children's book *The Snowy Day* about a dark-skinned boy named Peter enjoying winter. The book does not mention racial tensions as if they didn't exist in Peter's world. They likely do, as the book is by an American author and so probably takes place in the United States (although specific geographic indicators are absent). Can we consider as a serious limitation the fact that the colorful illustrations mostly shows the boy sliding off snow mounds, musing on his blue footprints, and making snow angels? Every author tells a story from the perspective she prefers for one reason or another. It may be something she knows best, believes in firmly, wants others to accept, or thinks her target audience would prefer (among other reasons). Most of the time, omissions are not something to hold against the storyteller.

A good exercise in critical thinking would be to imagine what could be said but was not, and to wonder why, without judging the author for his choices. One easy way to think about this is through the idea of unanswered questions. When you are watching a film or reading a book, imagine that you can ask their authors anything you want. If you are not shy, I am sure you can come up with many versions of "How about this?" and "Why did it happen that way?" In most cases, you won't have the luxury of addressing an actual person, but it's a known truism that formulating a good question can be as crucial as getting a definitive response. Also, remember Roland Barthes' argument: we can assume that many authors themselves do not understand hidden aspects of their own narratives.

A similar activity can be done when we are dealing with media practices, channels, and spaces. In these cases, instead of looking at the plot and characters, we can consider such aspects as functionality and structure. Website navigation, available gameplay paths, or a schedule of a news channel can seem logical until we start wondering how they could be different. This is a good time to consider multiple hidden power relationships that shape the media industry. For example, we may want to ask how a news story makes it through different steps of a media channel hierarchy to its audience or who makes decisions about identity descriptors that users of social networks choose from when registering a new account.

Alternatively, we can pick a media tool and do some research on why it looks the way it does and how it could be changed. Questions about accessibility come to mind: we may realize that a person with a disability would struggle using it. In this case, the omitted aspect of a media form would be its orientation toward the target audience comprised of people without disabilities. If we do some digging around, we may discover many interesting facts about the journey that a specific communication tool has traveled to get its users. It's illuminating to learn about power struggles behind inventions that changed the way we learn and interact with each other.[26]

Of course, the hidden aspects we are looking for should be relevant and illuminating in one way or another. If we investigate important omissions in a history book, the question "Where are the unicorns?" will not take us far. To use the children's hiding game as an analogy, this direction will be totally "cold." However, it will be getting warmer once we ask something along the lines of, "If the history is told by winners, who are the silent losers in these stories and what would they say if they could talk?"[27] Not all inquiries will be equally valuable. On the other hand, relevancy is relative, so it is important to keep options for the directions of your investigation open.

To develop awareness about your own choices as a media creator, you can ask yourself what angle you have chosen for narratives, tools, spaces, or channels you are offering to the world. Since taken-for-granted omissions are as difficult to notice as hidden assumptions, it's good to listen to other people's interpretations. "How about this?" can indicate curiosity and should not be interpreted as an intention to start a conflict. If you keep your ears open, you will hear many criticisms, and some of them will be harsher than others. Without being overwhelmed by them, you can use other people's perspectives to clarify and enrich your messages or improve practices you promote.

The set of five media literacy questions I discuss here is only one of the multiple paths toward achieving awareness and self-awareness when it comes to communication. I invite my readers to explore these other paths on their own. The key thing to remember is that having superior knowledge involves accepting that you will never know everything. Intellectual humility is better than the certitude that there is nothing else to discover.

EMPATHY: NONVIOLENT COMMUNICATION AND MINDFULNESS

In case I have given you an impression of being very good at empathy, my sincere apologies. Empathy is my ideal, but, in all honesty, I fail to follow this aspiration on a daily basis. The room for improvement seems like an infinite space. So how can I claim to help my readers hone a skill I don't fully possess? The idea of mindfulness may provide an effective comparison.[28]

If you have ever done mindfulness meditation, you know that the goal is not to stop thinking, judging, and feeling entirely. To succeed, you would have to be a corpse. The objective is to become self-aware enough to control your reactions without getting overwhelmed by this awareness. In the process, you will need to catch your mind again and again and *again* as it is trying to trick you. This struggle never ends. Even those who teach mindfulness will need to keep learning about it for the rest of their lives. Likewise, you don't have to completely block your negative feelings about other people and their actions when practicing empathy. You can be experiencing these emotions and at the same time training your mind to perceive a picture bigger than the immediate reaction (blame) will push you to accept. Empathy will probably never get easy, but it's worth doing anyway. When we are mindful, we can stay in the present—listening attentively instead of making definitive statements about ourselves and others. Empathy can help you achieve a very similar result.

One can find many books and other resources that contain guidelines for mindfulness meditation. Is there anything like that for empathy? I am happy to report that I have found a tool that provides specific steps one can take to work on this skill. Called Nonviolent Communication (NVC), it was developed by psychologist and mediator Marshall Rosenberg in the 1960s.[29]

He is the immediate author of the technique I am going to describe below, but is he the *only* author? Before Rosenberg, the principle of nonviolence was successfully applied by Martin Luther King Jr. as part of the civil rights movement. King learned about it from the Quaker activist Bayard Rustin, who was inspired by the Indian lawyer Mahatma Gandhi, who borrowed the idea from the Russian novelist Leo Tolstoy, whose major influence was the abolitionist William Lloyd Garrison.[30] It may be impossible to find specific names beyond that point in the past but one can be sure that throughout the human history, many different people believed that love conquers hate and acted on this conviction. The NVC approach is not entirely unique, neither is it a perfect fix for any problem.[31] But it's a good place to start.

The first key premise of NVC is that our minds are filled with judgments that color the language we choose to communicate. You may recognize a connection to what we have discussed on the previous pages: people live in worlds of subjective meanings that get expressed through various media forms. The problem with judgments is that they often prevent us from having a dialogue with each other. When you feel criticized, chances are you will not listen to your opponent because you will be too busy getting defensive. As a result, what you will say to her will likely reflect your judgment about that person, and the vicious cycle of blame will continue.

People don't even have to interact face-to-face in order to run into the same wall. We often form an enemy image (as Rosenberg called it) of somebody without ever being in one room with them. We think it's enough to know who the other person voted for or what social policies they support in order to fully understand who they are. So if we do get to interact with them in person or via modern technologies, this judgment is usually what they are going to hear loud and clear. Guess what they will say in response. In order to break this cycle, we need to look for something very important that's omitted from what our adversaries tell us. This leads to the second key premise of NVC.

As we are trying to formulate the most logical response possible in order to get our point across to the person we are arguing with, we forget to consider several crucial things. Everybody shares basic human needs: connection, physical well-being, honesty, play, peace, autonomy, and meaning. For example, we all want to know that we matter or that there is a universal order one can maintain through correct actions. When people's needs are not met, they experience negative emotions that include different shades of fear, anger, irritation, disgust, confusion, disconnection, embarrassment, sadness, tension, and yearning. According to proponents of NVC, we should learn to notice these unspoken feelings and needs behind what other people say and do.[32] If we try to persuade somebody by appealing to their reason, but ignoring their emotions and needs, we are probably going to fail. People do not make judgments solely based on logic.[33]

Same as we don't read between the lines—literally and metaphorically—when it comes to others' communicative acts, it's also easy to forget to put our own feelings and needs into words. We tell our kids: "It's stupid to act this way because you can hurt yourself" instead of "I am afraid when you are doing this because I need to know that you are safe." Words perceived as judgments come to us more readily than honest expression of emotions. Remember that blame is human mind's natural reaction to discomfort. In contrast, putting feeling into words requires vulnerability, which we often avoid because it seems counterintuitive. Vulnerability promises to create even more discomfort than we are already experiencing.

The solution, according to Rosenberg, lies in following four steps when we are trying to express ourselves and the same four steps when we are listening to others. First, we should learn to notice judgments and replace them with neutral *observations*. If you are the one speaking, put your observations into words. If you deal with words or actions of others, try to imagine their experiences. Second, we need to search our hearts for *feelings* and articulate them as clearly as we can—or listen to feelings behind other people's words, no matter how hurtful they may be. Third, we should look even deeper and connect negative feelings to *needs* that have not been met. At this point, a meaningful dialogue can finally happen. The fourth and final step is *requesting* to have our needs met or clarifying requests others are trying to make. Listening empathically and expressing ourselves honestly are, therefore, two sides of the NVC model.[34]

A skillful peacemaker, Rosenberg dealt with marital disagreements, family feuds, and conflicts between violent urban gangs. He traveled to war-torn areas around the world where he taught people who had experienced death and destruction to liberate themselves from enemy images that kept the war going. Conflict resolution is considered part of interpersonal communication, but I believe that the model of NVC is as relevant for interactions mediated by technology as it is for face-to-face conversations.

We can form a judgment about somebody before ever meeting them, without even knowing that this specific person exists, just because they are seen as part of a certain group. We can make sweeping statements about this group using online social networks, where the person we have never met will find our words and make judgments about us and a group he attributes us to. Digital social networks are amazing in their ability to connect people all around the world, but when we use them for awareness disconnected from empathy, they can breed angry mobs engaged in ugly blame wars.

Reasoning along the lines of "They started it first" and "Why should we be nice to them if they are mean to us?" seems legitimate when we believe that these conflicts are beyond our control. One of the most difficult aspects of empathy—the initial step that makes it possible—is simply having faith that it can help. To be honest, you may have to work very hard before you see any indication that it is working. As I previously confessed to you, it is my biggest bias to believe that we must keep pushing for empathy because eventually everybody will be rewarded. NVC in this sense is not perfect because it does not guarantee immediate results.

The lesson taught by Martin Luther King Jr. suggests that empathy does not have to be toothless. Same as Rosenberg, King talked about the importance of listening to people we see as our enemies, but he also called his followers to fight against power imbalances that prevent a true dialogue from happening. Obviously, if one side cannot get heard, there can be no meaningful conversation and no real conflict resolution. But demanding equality and using NVC are not mutually exclusive. We do not need to humiliate our enemies as we are looking for justice.[35] Unfortunately, below-the-belt communication tactics have become a distinctive feature of online debates. And because there are so many participants involved, more than just a few of them need to start practicing empathy for the overall climate of online arguments to improve.

If you have never heard of NVC before, my advice is to use it little by little but to do so consistently. Otherwise, you may soon burn out and will not trust this approach anymore, especially if the conflict keeps going. Do not force yourself to put feelings and needs into words every time you communicate. Sometimes it is enough simply to clarify in your own head why you are reacting in a certain way or why your opponents may behave the way they do. In the process, you will be able to slow down and reflect before you react. Here is a parallel with mindfulness again. Meditation can help us in conflict situations because it provides a mental pause button. By hitting it, we give ourselves time to observe the situation and our own emotions slowly and then choose the best course of action.[36]

You do not have to always follow the exact formula offered by Rosenberg since it may start getting repetitive. But once in a while, you can do all the steps in order to develop a mental habit of taking this route instead of plunging into blame. If you spend a lot of time on social media, this can be a good place to start. As you swipe through the messages, notice when you encounter anything that triggers especially strong negative emotions. You may immediately feel an urge to respond to messages that enrage you or to share a maddening story of injustice. This is the time to hit pause, let yourself breathe and observe. Replace statements like "This is outrageous!" or "What an idiot!" with more nuanced reactions that will include a neutral (or as neutral as possible) account of what happened. Then open the list of feelings and needs to find more profound explanations for what is going in your own head. Then do your best—and I know it will be extremely hard!—to consider feelings and needs of people on the "other side." You do not even have to get to the last stage of the NVC model—requesting. This one you may keep for in-person interactions.

When people find their mind getting repeatedly distracted during mediation, they think they have failed, and give up. Like any learning and growth, meditation is about failing and starting again. Same is empathy. You will be getting angry, frustrated, depressed, and frightened when you hear about injustices of the world. I surely hope you will, because if you won't it means you simply do not care! Your mind will be searching again and again for a guilty party, pushing you to make judgments about people you don't really know, seducing you with the easy solution of blame. The more tired and stressed you are, the quicker you will let these temptations carry you away. Do not let these obstacles stop you. Even if you let yourself get into *ad hominem* arguments once in a while, in the grand scheme of things you can still be following the path of nonviolence. You can remain aware of society's imperfections but see them through the lens of empathy. If you manage to do this at least sometimes, you will be ready for the culminating stage or the ACE model.

COLLABORATION: PIECES OF A PUZZLE

In 2015, U.S. television show "Saturday Night Live" featured a sketch titled *A Thanksgiving Miracle*. Created close to the time of November festivities, the scene portrays an extended family around the Thanksgiving table. The only thing that can keep them from fighting about controversial issues is the record-breaking single "Hello" by Adele, released a month prior to the airing of the sketch. Saturday Night Live offered a comment on the issue of polarization with its hallmark goofiness. As each family member turns into a grotesque version of Adele and participates in lip syncing the song (presumably, in their heads), the group is able to finish the dinner without jumping down each other's throats. The conflict is, thus, resolved not through dialogue but through self-isolation.

In the words of primatologist and scholar of animal behavior Frans de Waal, "the ability to function in a group and build a support network is a crucial survival skill."[37] This does not mean that we should always disregard our personal interest in favor of helping others. On the contrary, de Waal argued that the best society would be the one where individuals have found a balance between selfishness and selflessness. We just need to know how to support our community in a way that benefits us in the process. When a particular culture finds itself in the throes of polarization, it is moving away from this desirable state. The book by de Waal that I took the quote from is actually about empathy, which should give us a clue regarding strategies we should use to overcome resentment at least toward our own kin.[38]

Surely, there is already plenty of collaboration going on in the human society. Members of the *Homo sapiens* team are wired to set and achieve common goals together.[39] Yet, there is a big difference between surviving as a species and creating a well-balanced society where everybody's needs are met (most of the time). And we should not just assume that figuring out how to play nice in the global sandbox is other people's job. Yes, we should understand how modern technology has changed our lives. But if all we do is blame this technology and people who created it—instead of finding ways to strengthen our social bonds—we won't get too far.[40]

Of course, collaboration is not always possible. If somebody is literally holding a knife to your throat, it is totally understandable if you decide that you do not have time to deeply engage with this person's narrative (even though she undoubtedly has a complicated story to tell) and choose to protect yourself by any means necessary. Unfortunately, we often refuse to make any attempt to initiate collaboration through empathy even if we are not in such a dramatic situation.

Thanksgiving family gatherings in the United States are a good example of a situation when people whose life is not in any immediate danger choose the route of self-isolation or direct confrontation rather than work out their disagreements. Interestingly, the reasoning people give for avoiding empathy is that issues they disagree about are a matter of life and death. I think we should be more careful with such dramatic statements. They do not allow us to notice where collaboration built on deeper understanding of the "other side" is possible.

Only when people feel heard, they can begin to consider information that does not fit their preconceived notions. But if nobody decides to leave their comfort zone and listen to the other side without the feeling of moral superiority, there will be no conversation. Who will be the one to make the first step even before their own need for connection is truly met? That may seem like an unfair burden, but considering what's at stake may inspire you to try. If you are brave enough to practice empathy while expressing yourself honestly and vulnerably, the model of Nonviolent Communication will serve for your guidance. Once we have expanded horizons of our awareness and learned to talk to each other without merely hearing ourselves, we should be ready for the final stage: working together toward a better future for all.

Unfortunately, I do not have a specific strategy to offer to my readers for completing this last and the most crucial part of the journey. Awareness and empathy are (relatively) easy because they are something each individual can practice on their own. But collaboration, by the very definition, requires a concerted effort of multiple participants. Moreover, I am not talking simply about improving dynamics within one team, a large company, or even a country. The question that's left to answer is: How can *all* people around the globe work better with each other, without prioritizing anybody's experiences, voices, and truths?

Society, as we discussed in Chapter 4, is such an unwieldy beast that even trying to imagine it makes our brains hurt. Introducing the concept of macropower was one way to explain that no individual working on her own can ever change the direction where this creature of creatures is going. Throughout this book, I have argued that nobody has access to one objective and universal truth. It would not make any sense if I—a tiny speck of dust in the vast social universe—would dare to propose something that can help all the other specks swirl together in a more efficient way. I don't have a plan, and sometimes I feel confused and lost. But I know that this kind of vulnerability is key both for awareness (I don't know everything) and empathy (my own flaws are as inevitable as other people's imperfections). That's why this last section will not contain any instructions—only invitations.

I am inviting you to see yourself and others as pieces of a puzzle. To think of it, society is kind of like a big family: we are all in this together. One condition that must be fulfilled for a family unit not only to exist but also to thrive is that all members should feel seen and significant. Arguments will happen and once in a while storms of negative emotions will rage. They will not flip this boat if it's made on the basis of understanding and respect. Same as in any family, everybody cannot be happy all the time. Human beings constantly want a lot of things, which is a blessing and a curse. But what we all really need is connection, and the real deep connection can only exist if we acknowledge our mutual interdependence.

I am inviting you not to settle on easy solutions. No simplification will allow you to take into consideration multiple contradictory realities at once. We cannot start prioritizing truths, even though sometimes we can prioritize issues. Even if we do that, we cannot say: "This is the only real problem and nothing else matters before it is solved." This just won't work in the world where everybody and everything depends on each other. Somehow, we must learn to tackle it all at once, including things you personally worry about daily, those hidden from your sight, and those you don't even believe in (if others do, there is a reason for that).

I am inviting you to harness the power of media understood as people communicating with each other through technology. Communication is essential for the survival of our species. Like cells in the body of society, we need interactions between all the parts to flow smoothly in order for the whole to exist. Yet, social problems are reinforced through communication same as some diseases can be made worse by the natural circulation inside the human body. Although in this sense media can contribute to social problems, it is not their source. We need media literacy, which I understand as mindfulness in our communication practices. At the same time, the focus on advantages and limitations of the most recent technologies should not distract us from recognizing the fundamental principles of human communication rooted in the human nature. Seen through these principles, media can be used for enhancing our awareness and practicing empathy, instead of for swimming in our filter bubbles filled with blame toward everybody on the outside.

It's only through collaboration of the highest order—the one built on profound awareness intertwined with empathy—that the meandering flow of social change can take the most advantageous course. But a better future won't come in a form of an effortless kumbaya. There will always be struggles caused by the paradoxes of our humanity. Some of these struggles will take place *between* people, and others will happen *within* them. It does not mean that we will have to be stressed and miserable all the time, yet complacency has proven to be a kiss of death for any positive change. Being overly satisfied, slow, dismissive of looming dangers—I am sure my readers don't want to become the next dodo. For the sake of survival, we cannot expect to stay in our comfort zones forever.

Since you may be still wondering if this kind of collaboration can ever work when truly controversial issues are involved, I want to finish with a story. It's about one of the most divisive topics in the United States: abortion. In 1994, a deadly shooting in two women's health clinics in Massachusetts took place, shaking people on both sides of the debate. In the aftermath, Boston-based national group that facilitates difficult dialogues (now named Essential Partners) invited six leaders from the pro-choice and pro-life communities to have several off-the-record meetings. Initially apprehensive, the participants ended up spending more than 150 hours conversing with each other in person over the period of five-and-a-half years. As a result, they coauthored an article titled "Talking with the Enemy" that was published by the *Boston Globe* in 2001.[41]

The title is, in fact, deceptive. As the meetings progressed, the participants found it hard to keep seeing each other merely as adversaries. This was "an experience that has astonished us," they wrote. Their account is worth reading in full because it is both compelling and counterintuitive. Here I want to quote its concluding paragraphs that I find particularly thought-provoking:

These conversations revealed a deep divide. We saw that our differences on abortion reflect two world views that are irreconcilable.

If this is true, then why do we continue to meet?

First, because when we face our opponent, we see her dignity and goodness. Embracing this apparent contradiction stretches us spiritually. We've experienced something radical and life-altering that we describe in nonpolitical terms: "the mystery of love," "holy ground," or simply, "mysterious." [This is empathy. – E.F.]

We continue because we are stretched intellectually, as well. This has been a rare opportunity to engage in sustained, candid conversations about serious moral disagreements. It has made our thinking sharper and our language more precise. [This is awareness. – E.F.]

We hope, too, that we have become wiser and more effective leaders. We are more knowledgeable about our political opponents. We have learned to avoid being overreactive and disparaging to the other side and to focus instead on affirming our respective causes.

Since that first fear-filled meeting, we have experienced a paradox. While learning to treat each other with dignity and respect, we all have become firmer in our views about abortion.

We hope this account of our experience will encourage people everywhere to consider engaging in dialogues about abortion and other protracted disputes. In this world of polarizing conflicts, we have glimpsed a new possibility: a way in which people can disagree frankly and passionately, become clearer in heart and mind about their activism, and, at the same time, contribute to a more civil and compassionate society.

I realize that, while for some readers this may be an inspiring example of a civic dialogue, others will be left confused. We tend to think that the point of an argument is to make the other side accept our position as the ultimate truth. It seems logical that, if there is no agreement, collaboration is impossible. How can we do something together if no consensus has been reached?

The readers may point out that abortion still remains a divisive issue in the United States, although the attempt to have a dialogue described in the article was made back in the 1990s. Does this mean that it failed and the approach I advocate for does not work?

I remind you that the abortion debate is intrinsically connected to the political polarization, which is situated within the web of numerous controversial issues.[42] The abortion debate involves a good many individuals. If six of them (the authors of the article) were able to have a conversation based on empathy and awareness, this does not mean that the path to collaboration for everybody involved has been found. The insights of the participants can be used as an inspiration for creating more bridges, but many more people need to use this model in order for a visible change to happen.

Collaboration does not have to be based on the unification of opinions. It's about finding a new approach that none of the sides has envisioned. Prioritizing one truth over all others is an easy thing to do in the short run. Because it involves diminishing beliefs and values of our opponents, a conflict that is forced into hiding will eventually burst to the surface. In contrast, finding answers that lie beyond binaries may seem like an insurmountable task. By embarking on this quest, we commit to putting considerable effort *now* in order to fashion a more sustainable balance for the future. This prospect is daunting and the path in front of us is far from clear. Still, I believe that there is hope. Once we stop searching for easy solutions, we may find ourselves in front of endless possibilities.

NOTES

1. This definition comes from Lexico, the online version of Oxford Dictionary.

2. I borrowed the term "crushing certainty" from Lawrence Wright. He used it in the documentary *Going Clear: Scientology and the Prison of Belief* based on the book *Going Clear: Scientology, Hollywood and the Prison of Belief* (2013).

3. You may recognize my wording as a paraphrase of the famous verse "For with much wisdom comes much sorrow; the more knowledge, the more grief" (Ecclesiastes 1:18).

4. My understanding of media literacy comes from such scholars and practitioners as Cyndy Scheibe and Faith Rogow (2012), as well as Renee Hobbs (2021)—to name a few.

5. This definition is from Oxford Languages.

6. Obviously, awareness about media can be enhanced in many different ways. The tool I discuss in this section is merely one of them. I chose it because of its concreteness (specific questions), as well as due to my familiarity with it.

7. For instance, there are sets of questions proposed by Project Look Sharp, Center for Media Literacy, and National Association for Media Literacy Education.

8. For more information on the Media Literacy Smartphone, visit the website of the Media Education Lab (https://mediaeducationlab.com).

9. The phrase "The medium is the message" was first introduced in McLuhan's *Understanding Media: The Extensions of Man*, published in 1964.

10. This printout does look like an actual smartphone with the questions on the screen and additional tips for analyzing media on the other side.

11. Hayes (2018).

12. Barthes (1977).

13. Some believe that, to win these battles, attention is to be treated as a limited resource and economic theory must be applied to find effective strategies of managing it. This approach is called "attention economy" (Davenport & Beck, 2001).

14. This is what makes propaganda effective (Hobbs, 2020).

15. It is probably connected to properties of our cognition that determine our tendency to look for patterns, order, and meaning (discussed in Chapter 2 of the current volume).

16. This structure was first described back in the Ancient Greece by Aristotle, who provided the basis of the narrative theory in his *Poetics* approximately 335 BC (see Aristotle as reprinted in 2020).

17. For more information on this approach, described as "SUCCESs model," by Chip and Dan Heath, see their book *Made to Stick: Why Some Ideas Survive and Others Die* (2007).

18. Hobbs (2020).

19. This Greek philosopher was allegedly concerned that writing will weaken people's minds by negatively affecting their memory (see Ong, 2002).

20. As of 2020, the video has been viewed by over 25 million people (Pro Infirmis, 2013).

21. The following analysis is taken from the article that I published with my colleague Donnell Probst (Friesem & Probst, 2020).

22. The assumption that one can speak for the whole group he or she belongs may lead to the so-called "burden of representation" (see Mercer, 1990).

23. Instead of protecting students from harmful influence of the modern media, teachers and parents can empower young people to learn through their creativity (Hobbs, 2017).

24. When my liberal friends and students tell me that they have no idea how they could possibly understand somebody who is republican, I often recommend them to read a thought-provoking book by Arlie Russell Hochschild *Strangers in Their Own Land: Anger and Mourning on the American Right* (2016).

25. Heath and Heath (2006).

26. For instance, Thomas Edison, who influenced many modern media practices, was a ruthless businessman often warring with contemporary inventors. See Morris (2019).

27. It may be useful to ask this question of all history books and textbooks, no matter how many people agree with facts provided in them (Loewen, 2018).

28. Kabat-Zinn (2016).

29. See Rosenberg 2015, and the website of The Center for Nonviolent Communication (https://www.cnvc.org).

30. To learn more about the history of nonviolence, listen to podcast series The Thread, season three.

31. I personally think that looking for easy fixes is in general useless, if not dangerous, thing to do. NVC is a great tool, but applying it is not easy—in my experience, even to seemingly simple family disagreements. The human society has been torn by major conflicts as long as it has existed. Some of them can be even classified as "the five percent conflicts," as Peter Coleman (2011) suggests. These disagreements are the most difficult ones to overcome, and while they can be understood better when we use principles of NVC, this does not make them easy to get rid of. It's always good to explore other possible strategies without looking for

a silver bullet. For a possible alternative, see the book *Crucial Conversations* by Patterson et al. (2011).

32. To find the complete list of needs and feelings, visit a website of The Center for Nonviolent Communication (https://www.cnvc.org).

33. See the elephant metaphor developed by Jonathan Haidt in *The Happiness Hypothesis* (2007) and *The Righteous Mind* (2012).

34. The model of NVC involves expressing ourselves honestly and listening to others empathically as we take into consideration our own and other people's feelings and needs. For a visual representation of the model, visit the website of The Center for Nonviolent Communication (https://www.cnvc.org).

35. According to Martin Luther King Jr., six steps of nonviolent social change include direct action, which is necessary when your opponent refuses to listen to you and uses their power to oppress you. However, the culminating stage of this model is reconciliation: "Nonviolence seeks friendship and understanding with the opponent. Nonviolence does not seek to defeat the opponent . . . Through reasoned compromise, both sides resolve the injustice with a plan of action" (this quote was taken from website of The King Center).

36. Reflecting instead of reacting is one of the key ideas of mindfulness meditation.

37. de Waal (2009), p. 33.

38. I wrote "at least," but an argument can be made that being empathic toward our relatives is sometimes more difficult than navigating relationships with strangers.

39. We cannot survive without collaboration because our individual knowledge about the world will not be complete unless we rely on others (Sloman & Philip, 2017).

40. Rushkoff (2019).

41. Although originally published by *The Boston Globe*, the full text of the article can be now accessed through feminist.com (Fowler et al., 2001).

42. This is a typical example of the "five percent conflict" described by Coleman (2011).

Bibliography

Adelson, E.H. (1995). *Checkershadow illusion.* http://persci.mit.edu/gallery/check ershadow

Adorno, T., & Horkheimer, M. (2002[1947]). *Dialectic of Enlightenment* (E. Jephcott, Trans.). Stanford University Press.

Allport, G.W. (1954). *The nature of prejudice.* Addison-Wesley.

Anderson, G. (2013, October 22). Is Jeff Bezos a horrible boss and is that good? *Forbes.* https://www.forbes.com/sites/retailwire/2013/10/22/is-jeff-bezos-a-hor rible-boss-and-is-that-good

Anti-slavery (n.d.). *What is modern slavery?* https://www.antislavery.org/slavery -today/modern-slavery

Ariely, D. (2010). *Predictably irrational: The hidden forces that shape our decisions.* Harper Perennial.

Aristotle (2020). *Poetics* (S.H. Butcher, Trans.). Compass Circle.

Avineri, S. (1968). *The social and political thought of Karl Marx.* Cambridge University Press.

Banaji, M.R., & Greenwald, A.G. (2013). *Blindspot: Hidden biases of good people.* Delacorte Press.

Bandura, A. (1962). *Social learning through imitation.* University of Nebraska Press.

Barthes, R. (1977). The death of the author. In R. Barthes (Ed.), *Image-Music-Text* (S. Heath, Trans.) (pp. 142–148). Hill and Wang.

Behnken, B.D., & Smithers, J.D. (2015). *Racism in American popular media: From Aunt Jemima to the Frito Bandito.* Praeger.

Benjamin, W. (2019[1955]). The work of art in the age of mechanical reproduction (H. Zohn, Trans.). In H. Arendt (Ed.), *Illuminations: Essays and reflections* (pp. 166–195). First Mariner Books.

Berger, P.L., & Luckmann, T. (1967). *The social construction of reality: A treatise in the sociology of knowledge.* Anchor Books.

Berlo, D.K. (1960). *The process of communication: An introduction to theory and practice.* Holt, Rinehart and Winston.

Blair, A. (2003). Reading strategies for coping with information overload ca. 1550-1700. *Journal of the History of Ideas, 64*(1), 11–28.

Blumer, H. (1969). *Symbolic interactionism: Perspective and method*. University of California Press.

Blumler, J., & Katz, E. (1974). *The uses of mass communication: Current perspectives on gratification research*. Sage.

Bobo, J. (2002). The Color Purple: Black women as cultural readers. In R.R.M. Coleman (Ed.), *Say it loud!: African-American audiences, media, and identity* (pp. 205–228). Routledge.

Booker, C. (2019[2004]). *The seven basic plots: Why we tell stories*. Continuum.

boyd, d. (2010). Social network sites as networked publics: Affordances, dynamics, and implications. In Z. Papacharissi (Ed.), *Networked self: Identity, community, and culture on social network sites* (pp. 39–58). Routledge.

boyd, d. (2015). *It's complicated: The social lives of networked teens*. Yale University Press.

boyd, d. (2017). Did media literacy backfire? *Points: Data & Society*. https://points.datasociety.net/did-media-literacy-backfire-7418c084d88d

Bramlett-Solomon, S., & Carstarphen, M.G. (2014). *Race, gender, class, and media: Studying mass communication and multiculturalism* (2nd ed.). Kendall Hunt Publishing.

Brann, N.L. (1981). *The Abbot Trithemius (1462–1516): The Renaissance of monastic humanism*. Brill Academic Publishing.

Briggs, C.F., & Maverick, A. (2012[1923]). *The story of the telegraph, and a history of the great Atlantic cable: A complete record of the inception, progress, and final success of that undertaking*. Ulan Press.

Brown, B. (2010a). *The power of vulnerability* [TEDxHouston]. https://www.ted.com/talks/brene_brown_the_power_of_vulnerability

Brown, B. (2010b). *The gifts of imperfection: Let go of who you think you're supposed to be and embrace who you are*. Hazelden Publishing.

Brown, B. (2015). *Daring greatly: How the courage to be vulnerable transforms the way we live, love, parent, and lead*. Avery.

Brown, B. (2019). *Braving the wilderness: The quest for true belonging and the courage to stand alone*. Random House.

Bruns, A. (2008). *Blogs, Wikipedia, second life and beyond: From production to produsage*. Peter Lang.

Bruns, A. (2019). *Are filter bubbles real?* Polity.

Bryant, J., Thompson, S., & Finklea, B.W. (2012). *Fundamentals of media effects* (2nd ed.). Waveland Press.

Cain, A. (2017, November 14). 9 shocking anecdotes that reveal Jeff Bezos's cutthroat management style. *Inc*. https://www.inc.com/business-insider/amazon-ceo-jeff-bezos-leadership-management-style-work-culture.html

Carr, N. (2010). *The shallows: What the Internet is doing to our brains*. W.W. Norton & Company.

Chen, W. (2016, August 26). How not to create a toxic culture, courtesy of ex-Amazon employees. *Inc*. https://www.inc.com/walter-chen/four-lessons-in-building-a-culture-that-doesnt-suck-from-ex-amazon-employees.html

Cole, R. (1996). *Propaganda in twentieth century war and politics: An annotated bibliography.* Scarecrow Press.

Coleman, P. (2011). *The five percent: Finding solutions to seemingly impossible conflicts.* PublicAffairs.

Compaine, B.M. (2001). *The digital divide: Facing a crisis or creating a myth?* MIT Press.

Cooley, C.H. (1998[1902]). *On self and social organization.* University of Chicago Press.

Crenshaw, K. (1989). Demarginalizing the intersection of race and sex: A Black feminist critique of antidiscrimination doctrine, feminist theory and antiracist politics. *University of Chicago Legal Forum, 1989*(1), 139–167.

Crockett, Z. (2019, April 13). 5-star phonies: Inside the fake Amazon review complex. *The Hustle.* https://thehustle.co/amazon-fake-reviews

Davenport, T., & Beck, J. (2001). *The attention economy: Understanding the new currency of business.* Harvard Business School Press.

Davis, E.E., & Wartella, E. (Eds.). (1996). *American communication research: The remembered history.* Lawrence Erlbaum.

de Andreis, F., & Carioni, M. (2019). Theoretical observations on power in complex organizations. *American Journal of Industrial and Business Management, 9,* 1423–1430.

de Waal, F. (2009). *The age of empathy: Nature's lessons for a kinder society.* Random House.

Edwards, J. (2013, October 22). "Sadistic" Amazon treated book sellers "the way a cheetah would pursue a sickly gazelle." *Business Insider.* https://www.business insider.com/sadistic-amazon-treated-book-sellers-the-way-a-cheetah-would-pu rsue-a-sickly-gazelle-2013-10

Eidelman, S., & Crandall, C.S. (2014). The intuitive traditionalist: How biases for existence and longevity promote the status quo. *Advances in Experimental Social Psychology, 50,* 53–104.

Feeney, M. (2018, May 31). Yes, Amazon is tracking people. *Washington Examiner.* https://www.washingtonexaminer.com/opinion/yes-amazon-is-tracking-people-an d-sending-their-data-to-police

Fisher, R., Ury, W.L., & Patton B. (2011[1981]). *Getting to yes: Negotiating agreement without giving in* (3rd ed.). Penguin Books.

Foucault, M. (1972). *The archeology of knowledge* (A.M. Sheridan Smith, Trans.). Pantheon.

Foucault, M. (1998[1976]). *The history of sexuality: The will to knowledge* (R. Hurley, Trans.). Penguin.

Fowler, A., Nichols Gamble, N., Hogan, F.X., Kogut, M., McCommish, M., & Thorp, B. (2001, January 28.). Talking with the enemy. *Boston Globe.* https://www.fem inist.com/resources/artspeech/genwom/talkingwith.html

Friedan, B. (2001[1963]). *The feminine mystique.* Norton.

Friesem, D.E., & Lavi, N. (2019). An ethnoarchaeological view on hunter-gatherer sharing and its archaeological implications for the use of social space. In N. Lavi & D.E. Friesem (Eds.), *Towards a broader view of hunter-gatherer sharing* (pp. 85–96). McDonald Institute Monographs Series.

Friesem, E., & Friesem, Y. (2019). Media literacy education in the era of post-truth: Paradigm crisis. In M. Yildiz, M. Fazal, M. Ahn, R. Feirsen, & S. Ozdemir (Eds.), *Handbook of research on media literacy research and applications across disciplines* (pp. 119–134). IGI Global.

Friesem, E., & Probst, D. (2020). Teaching about intersections of disability, gender, and sexuality through media literacy education. *Journal of Literacy and Technology, 21*(1), 2–29.

Garland-Thompson, R. (1997). *Extraordinary bodies: Figuring physical disability in American culture and literature.* Columbia University Press.

Gauntlett, D. (2005). *Moving experiences: Understanding television's influences and effects* (2nd ed.). Indiana University Press.

Geertz, C. (1973). *The interpretation of cultures.* Basic Books.

Gill, R. (2007). *Gender and the media.* Polity.

Gramsci, A., Hoare, Q., & Nowell-Smith, G. (1972). *Selections from the prison notebooks of Antonio Gramsci.* International Publishers.

Greene, J. (2020, April 14). Amazon fires two tech workers who criticized the company's warehouse workplace conditions. *The Washington Post.* https://www.washingtonpost.com/technology/2020/04/13/amazon-workers-fired

Griswold, A. (2018, November 29). How Amazon hijacked the baby registry. *Quartz.* https://qz.com/1478347/how-amazon-hijacked-the-baby-registry

Haidt, J. (2007). *The happiness hypothesis: Putting ancient wisdom and philosophy to the test of modern science.* Arrow Books.

Haidt, J. (2012). *The righteous mind: Why good people are divided by politics and religion.* Vintage Books.

Hall, S. (2003[1980]). *Culture, media, language: Working papers in cultural studies, 1972–1979.* Routledge.

Harari, Y.N. (2015). *Sapiens: A brief history of humankind.* HarperCollins Publishers.

Harvey, A. (2019). *Feminist media studies.* Polity Press.

Havel, V. (1985). *The power of the powerless* (P. Wilson, Trans.). In J. Keane (Ed.). *The power of the powerless* (pp. 23–96). M.E. Sharpe.

Hayek, S. (2017, December 12). Harvey Weinstein is my monster too. The *New York Times.* https://www.nytimes.com/interactive/2017/12/13/opinion/contributors/salma-hayek-harvey-weinstein.html

Hayes, M. (2018, September 13). Who invented the iPhone? *Scientific American.* https://blogs.scientificamerican.com/observations/who-invented-the-iphone

Heath, C., & Heath, D. (2006). The curse of knowledge. *Harvard Business Review.* https://hbr.org/2006/12/the-curse-of-knowledge

Heath, C., & Heath, D. (2007). *Made to stick: Why some ideas survive and others die.* Random House.

Herrman, J. (2011, January 31). Why Nielsen ratings are inaccurate, and why they'll stay that way. *Vulture.* https://www.vulture.com/2011/01/why-nielsen-ratings-are-inaccurate-and-why-theyll-stay-that-way.html

Hickmann, M. (2000). Linguistic relativity and linguistic determinism: Some new directions. *Linguistics, 38*(2), 409–434.

Higdon, N. (2020). *The anatomy of fake news: Critical news literacy education.* University of California Press.

Hobbs, R. (2017). *Create to learn: Introduction to digital literacy.* Wiley Blackwell.

Hobbs, R. (2020). *Mind over media: Propaganda education for a digital age.* W.W. Norton & Company.

Hobbs, R. (2021). *Media literacy in action: Questioning the media.* Rowman & Littlefield.

Hobbs, R., & Jensen, A. (2009). The past, present, and future of media literacy education. *The Journal of Media Literacy Education, 1*(1), 1–11.

Hochschild, A.R. (2016). *Strangers in their own land: Anger and mourning on the American right.* The New Press.

Hopkins, D.J., & Ladd, J.M. (2014). The consequences of broader media choice: Evidence from the expansion of Fox News. *Quarterly Journal of Political Science, 9*, 115–135.

Inzlicht, M., & Schmader, T. (2011). *Stereotype threat: Theory, process, and application.* Oxford University Press.

Isenberg, N. (2017). *White trash: The 400-year untold history of class in America.* Penguin Books.

Jenkins, H. (1992). *Textual poachers: Television fans & participatory culture.* Routledge.

Jenkins, H. (2006). *Convergence culture: Where old and new media collide.* NYU Press.

Jenkins, H., Purushotma, R., Weigel, M., Clinton, K., & Robison, A.J. (2009). *Confronting the challenges of participatory culture: Media education for the 21st century.* The MIT Press.

Jeong, M. (2018, August 13). "Everybody immediately knew that it was for Amazon": Has Bezos become more powerful in D.C. than Trump? *Vanity Fair.* https://www.vanityfair.com/news/2018/08/has-bezos-become-more-powerful-in-dc-than-trump

Jung, C. (1953). Psychology and alchemy (G. Adler, Trans.). In C. Jung (Ed.), *Collected works* (Vol. 12). Princeton University Press.

Kabat-Zinn, J. (2016). *Mindfulness for beginners: Reclaiming the present moment and your life.* Sounds True.

Kahneman, D. (2013). *Thinking, fast and slow.* Farrar, Straus and Giroux.

Kay, A.C., Gaucher, D., Peach, J.M., Laurin, K., Friesen, J., Zanna, M.P., & Spencer, S.J. (2009). Inequality, discrimination, and the power of the status quo: Direct evidence for a motivation to see the way things are as the way they should be. *Journal of Personality and Social Psychology, 97*(3), 421–434.

King, M.L. (2010). *Strength to love.* Fortress Press.

KnowTheChain. (n.d.) *Company List.* https://knowthechain.org/company-lists

Lafrance, A. (2014, July 28). In 1858, people said the telegraph was "too fast for the truth." Sound familiar? *The Atlantic.* https://www.theatlantic.com/technology/archive/2014/07/in-1858-people-said-the-telegraph-was-too-fast-for-the-truth/375171

Lasswell, H.D., Casey, R.D., & Smith, B.L. (Eds.). (1935). *Propaganda and promotional activities: An annotated bibliography.* The University of Chicago Press.

Lazarsfeld, P.F., Berelson, B., & Gaudet, H. (1944). *The people's choice: How the voter makes up his mind in a presidential campaign*. Columbia University Press.

Leeds-Hurwitz, W. (1993). *Semiotics and communication: Signs, codes, cultures* (3rd ed.). Lawrence Erlbaum Associates.

Levine-Weinberg, A. (2018, October 14). Amazon could have a very real antitrust problem. *The Motley Fool*. https://www.fool.com/investing/2018/10/14/amazon-c ould-have-a-very-real-antitrust-problem.aspx

Lewis, J. (2016). *Media, culture, and human violence: From savage lovers to violent complexity*. Rowman & Littlefield.

Lippmann, W. (1922). *Public opinion*. Harcourt, Brace and Company.

Loewen, J. (2018). *Lies my teacher told me: Everything your American history textbook got wrong*. The New Press.

Loftus, E., & Ketcham, K. (2013). *The myth of repressed memory: False memories and allegations of sexual abuse*. Griffin.

Lopez, G. (2017, May 7). For years, this popular test measured anyone's racial bias. But it might not work after all. *Vox*. https://www.vox.com/identities/2017/3/7/ 14637626/implicit-association-test-racism

Lowery, S.A., & DeFleur, M.L. (1983). *Milestones of mass communication research: Media effects*. Longman.

Mahler, J., & Rutenberg, J. (2019, April 3). How Rupert Murdoch's empire of influence remade the world. The *New York Times*. https://www.nytimes.com/intera ctive/2019/04/03/magazine/rupert-murdoch-fox-news-trump.html

Mason, L. (2018). *Uncivil agreement: How politics became our identity*. University of Chicago Press.

Masterman, L. (1985). *Teaching the media*. Routledge.

Matsakis, L. (2018, September 6). The truth about Amazon, food stamps, and tax breaks. *Wired*. https://www.wired.com/story/truth-about-amazon-food-stamps-tax -breaks

Matsakis, L. (2019, September 9). Amazon employees will walk out over the company's climate change inaction. *Wired*. https://www.wired.com/story/amazon- walkout-climate-change

Meehan, E. (2005). *Why TV is not our fault: Television programming, viewers, and who's really in control*. Rowman & Littlefield.

Mercer, K. (1990). Black art and the burden of representation. *Third Text, 4*(10), 61–78.

McIntosh, P. (1990). White privilege: Unpacking the invisible knapsack. *Independent School, 49*(2), 31–35.

McLuhan, M. (1964). *Understanding media*. Mentor.

McRaney, D. (2012). *You are not so smart: Why you have too many friends on Facebook, why your memory is mostly fiction, and 46 other ways you're deluding yourself*. Gotham Books.

Mind over media (n.d.). *Learn*. https://propaganda.mediaeducationlab.com/learn

Morris, E. (2019). *Edison*. Random House.

Nicholson, C. (2018). *Fake news: It's your fault* [TedXBocaRaton]. https://www.ted .com/talks/christina_nicholson_fake_news_it_s_your_fault

Noble, S.U. (2018). *Algorithms of oppression: How search engines reinforce racism.* New York University Press.

Nöth, W. (1995). *Handbook of semiotics.* Indiana University Press.

Ogunyemi, L. (2017, October 10). I am the woman in the "racist Dove ad": I am not a victim. *The Guardian.* https://www.theguardian.com/commentisfree/2017/oct/10/i-am-woman-racist-dove-ad-not-a-victim

Ong, W.J. (2002). *Orality and literacy.* Routledge.

Paglia, C. (1990, December 14). Madonna – finally, a real feminist. The *New York Times.* https://www.nytimes.com/1990/12/14/opinion/madonna-finally-a-real-feminist.html

Pariser, A. (2012). *The filter bubble: How the new personalized web is changing what we read and how we think.* Penguin Books.

Patterson, K., Grenny, J., McMillan, R., & Switzler, A. (2011). *Crucial conversations: Tools for talking when stakes are high* (2nd ed.). McGraw-Hill Education.

Pease, B., & Pease, A. (2006). *The definitive book of body language: The hidden meaning behind people's gestures and expressions.* Bantam.

Perry, A., & Shamay-Tsoory, S. (2013). Understanding emotional and cognitive empathy: A neuropsychological perspective. In S. Baron-Cohen, H. Tager-Flusberg, & Lombardo, M.V. (Eds.), *Understanding other minds: Perspectives from developmental social neuroscience* (pp.178–194). Oxford University Press.

Peterson, H. (2018, September 11). Missing wages, grueling shifts, and bottles of urine: The disturbing accounts of Amazon delivery drivers may reveal the true human cost of "free" shipping. *Business Insider.* https://www.businessinsider.com/amazon-delivery-drivers-reveal-claims-of-disturbing-work-conditions-2018-8

Plato. (2018). *The Republic* (B. Jowett, Trans.). Clydesdale.

Porter, J. (2018, October 2). Amazon raises minimum wage to $15 for all 350,000 US workers following criticism. *The Verge.* https://www.theverge.com/2018/10/2/17927478/amazon-minimum-wage-15-dollars-increase-bernie-sanders

Postman, N. (1985). *Amusing ourselves to death: Public discourse in the age of show business.* Penguin.

Potter, W.J. (2014). A critical analysis of cultivation theory. *Journal of Communication, 64*(6), 1015–1036.

Pro Infirmis. (2013, December 2). Pro Infirmis "Because who is perfect?" [YouTube video]. https://www.youtube.com/watch?v=E8umFV69fNg&ab_channel=ProInfirmis

Rand, E. (1995). *Barbie's queer accessories.* Duke University Press.

Reimann, N. (2020, May 26). Amazon sent out a scripted news segment, and eleven stations aired it. *Forbes.* https://www.forbes.com/sites/nicholasreimann/2020/05/26/amazon-sent-out-a-scripted-news-segment-and-11-stations-aired-it/?sh=7e5940ac48b9

Roberts, J. (2017, December 11). Amazon drivers "forced to urinate in bottles to keep on top of deliveries." *Metro.* https://metro.co.uk/2017/12/11/amazon-drivers-forced-urinate-bottles-keep-top-deliveries-7151258

Rosenberg, M.B. (2015). *Nonviolent Communication: A language of life.* PuddleDancer Press.

Rothman, J. (2014, May 12). The origins of "privilege." The *New Yorker*. https://ww
w.newyorker.com/books/page-turner/the-origins-of-privilege

RSA. (2015, February 3). Brené Brown on blame. https://www.youtube.com/watch?
v=RZWf2_2L2v8&ab_channel=RSA

Rushkoff, D. (2019). *Team human*. W.W. Norton & Company.

Sardar, Z., & Van Loon, B. (1994). *Introducing cultural studies*. Totem Books.

Scheibe, C., & Rogow, F. (2012). *The teacher's guide to media literacy: Critical thinking in a multimedia world*. Corwin.

Schramm, W. (1973). *Men, messages, and media: A look at human communication*. Harper and Row.

Scott, J., & Carrington, P.J. (Eds.). (2011). *The SAGE handbook of social network analysis*. Sage.

Segran, E. (2018, December 14). Did a slave make your sneakers? The answer is: probably. *Fast Company*. https://www.fastcompany.com/90279693/did-a-slave-m
ake-your-sneakers-the-answer-is-probably

Sloman, S., & Fernbach, P. (2017). *The knowledge illusion: Why we never think alone*. Riverhead Books.

Soper, S. (2015, August 17). Inside Amazon's warehouse. *The Morning Call*. https
://www.mcall.com/news/watchdog/mc-allentown-amazon-complaints-20110917
-story.html#

Statt, N. (2019, August 2). The FTC is looking into the Amazon and Apple deal that crushed small resellers. *The Verge*. https://www.theverge.com/2019/8/2/20751482
/ftc-amazon-apple-iphone-reseller-agreement-antitrust

Steele, M.A., Halkin, S.L., Smallwood, P.D., McKenna, T.J., Mitsopoulos, K., & Beam, M. (2008). Cache protection strategies of a scatter-hoarding rodent: Do tree squirrels engage in behavioural deception? *Animal Behaviour, 75*(2), 705–714.

Sternheimer, K. (2013). *Connecting social problems and popular culture: Why media is not the answer* (2nd ed.). Routledge.

Stone, B. (2013). *The everything store: Jeff Bezos and the age of Amazon*. Little, Brown and Company.

Streitfeld, D., & Haughney, C. (2013, August 17). Expecting the unexpected from Jeff Bezos. The *New York Times*. https://www.nytimes.com/2013/08/18/business/
expecting-the-unexpected-from-jeff-bezos.html

Suthivarakom, S. (2020, February 11). What to do if you think your Amazon purchase is a fake. *Wirecutter*. https://www.nytimes.com/wirecutter/blog/what-to-do-amaz
on-purchase-fake

The King Center (n.d.). *The King philosophy*. https://thekingcenter.org/the-king-ph
ilosophy

The Thread. (2018). *A history of nonviolence* (season 3) [Podcast]. https://www
.ozy.com/true-and-stories/listen-now-ozy-pulls-the-thread-on-the-nonviolence-mo
vement/89254

Toffler, A. (1980). *The third wave: The classic study of tomorrow*. Bantam.

Tuchman, G. (1978). The symbolic annihilation of women by the mass media. In G. Tuchman, A. Daniels, & J. Benet (Eds.), *Health and home: Images of women in the mass media* (pp. 3–38). Oxford University Press.

Turkle, S. (2017). *Alone together: Why we expect more from technology and less from each other.* Basic Books.

Turner, G. (2002). *British cultural studies: An introduction* (3rd ed.). Routledge.

van de Poel, I. (2011). The relation between forward-looking and backward-looking responsibility. In N. Vincent, I. van de Poel, & J. van den Hoven (Eds.), *Moral responsibility: Library of ethics and applied philosophy* (Vol. 27). Springer.

Vosoughi, S., Roy, D., & Aral, S. (2018). The spread of true and false news online. *Science, 359*(6380), 1146–1151.

Weinberg, H. (1959). *Levels of knowing and existence: Studies in general semantics.* Harper and Row.

Wood, C. (2020, May 4). Longtime Amazon VP Tim Bray just quit in dismay, calling the company "chickens---" for firing workers who criticized it. *Business Insider.* https://www.businessinsider.com/amazon-engineer-resigned-treatment-warehouse -whistleblowers-2020-5

Wright, L. (2013). *Going clear: Scientology, Hollywood and the prison of belief.* Alfred A. Knopf.

Index

About the Author

Elizaveta Friesem teaches in the Communication Department of Columbia College Chicago and is an affiliated faculty member of the Media Education Lab of the University of Rhode Island. An interdisciplinary scholar with an international background, Friesem works on problematizing common understandings of media, including its relationship to self, meaning, and power. She is also an editor of the *Journal of Media Literacy Education*.

www.ingramcontent.com/pod-product-compliance
Lightning Source LLC
Chambersburg PA
CBHW030652270326
41929CB00007B/335